THE TEN COMMANDMENTS
IN NEW PERSPECTIVE

STUDIES IN BIBLICAL THEOLOGY

A series of monographs designed to provide clergy and laymen with the best work in biblical scholarship both in this country and abroad

STUDIES IN BIBLICAL THEOLOGY

Second Series · 7

THE TEN COMMANDMENTS IN NEW PERSPECTIVE

A traditio-historical approach

EDUARD NIELSEN

SCM PRESS LTD

BLOOMSBURY STREET LONDON

Translated by David J. Bourke from the German
Die zehn Gebote: eine traditionsgeschichtliche Skizze
(Acta Theologica Danica VIII)
Prostant apud Munksgaard, Copenhagen, 1965

SBN 334 01612 6
FIRST PUBLISHED IN ENGLISH 1968
© SCM PRESS LTD 1968
PRINTED IN GREAT BRITAIN BY
ROBERT CUNNINGHAM AND SONS LTD
LONGBANK WORKS, ALVA

Contents

Contents

Foreword

THE Ten Commandments constitute beyond doubt the best known and most influential single passage in the whole Old Testament. It is remarkable therefore that until recently there have been very few books in English devoted especially to the understanding and interpretation of it and working with full competence within the recognized methods of modern Old Testament scholarship. Perhaps there is something in the English-speaking tradition of religious studies which has led people to expect little profit from the investigation of the law of ancient Israel. Among scholars, however, as Professor Nielsen points out, the study of Israelite law has in recent years become a very lively and creative subject. This present book is one among several which have recently appeared in English and presented to us the thoughts of Continental scholarship. Israelite law was not, as a superficial reading of the Old Testament might suggest, dropped complete from heaven, but grew and developed through various phases of the life of the Hebrew people. Professor Nielsen, following a wholesome direction which has been widely adopted in Scandinavia, seeks to look at all of these phases and not only the first or the last of them. His work will not fail to provoke some disagreement; but its fresh and stimulating character will be acknowledged by all. In the present climate of discussion within theology, in which a renewed importance is being attached to questions of ethics, a warm welcome will be accorded to this little book, which takes further the discussion in an earlier volume in this series.

JAMES BARR

Preface

THE traditio-historical sketch which follows derives for the most part from a series of lectures which I was invited to deliver in the spring of 1962 at the Swedish Theological Institute in Jerusalem. The subject was 'The Ten Commandments and Apodictic Law in the Old Testament'. These lectures were prepared on the basis of an independent study of the biblical texts without particular regard to the recent scholarly literature on the decalogue, which has gradually become extremely copious.

Since 1962 I have several times returned to the subject and have taken particular pains to acquaint myself with the latest researches. It can hardly cause surprise that these show signs of being strongly influenced by form-critical points of view, and that they are indebted to a quite overwhelming extent to two works: first to Sigmund Mowinckel's book *Le Décalogue*, 1927, second, and more particularly, to that of Albrecht Alt, *Die Ursprünge des israelitischen Rechts*, 1934. It is perhaps more remarkable that the work of form-criticism itself gave rise simultaneously to a renewal of theological interest in the decalogue, to fresh speculations concerning its date, and to a widening of orientation from the aspect of 'Religionsgeschichte'. In the intensely active research of the past five years the breaking up of old established positions is everywhere apparent. Fresh perspectives are opened up. The study of Israelite law, which for so many years led a shadowy existence, and indeed seems to have been almost totally neglected in favour of research into the rest of Old Testament literature, has today been drawn so much into the centre of interest that every survey of researches is already out of date as soon as it is published. I too must emphasize that any attempt at providing a detailed 'history of research' is quite beyond my intention. For this I can only refer those interested to two survey articles, 'Der Dekalog' by Ludwig Koehler (*TR*, NF1, 1929, pp. 161-184), and 'Dreissig

Jahre Dekalogforschung' by Johann Jakob Stamm (*TR*, NF 27, 1961, pp. 189-239 and 280-305), and to Stamm's book, *The Ten Commandments in Recent Research* (ET with additions by M. E. Andrew), 1967, as well as to the bibliographies provided in 'Moses and the Decalogue' by H. H. Rowley (*BJRL* 34, 1951, pp. 81-118), in *Études sur le Code de l'Alliance*, 1946, by H. Cazelles and in *Gebot und Predigt im Dekalog*, 1962, by Henning Graf Reventlow.

This work is described in the sub-title as 'A Traditio-historical Approach'. A mere approach makes no claim to give a survey from all angles of all that must have been published on its subject as the outcome of the previous generation's researches. Far less does it claim to have set out 'the definitive solution'. By the term 'traditio-historical' the author declares his adherence to a particular method of research. In its original form the material of the tradition under investigation was organically connected with a particular time and a particular place. As it now exists it has been separated from these and has become an element in a literary complex. Between these two stages in its development lie the numerous phases and epochs through which it has passed. It is taken that the special task of the traditio-historical approach is to trace the course of the material transmitted through these, examining each stage independently with the aim of determining its special interest, instead of (as happens all too often) concentrating exclusively upon the beginning and the end of the development.

INTRODUCTION

Of all the passages in the Old Testament the decalogue, 'the ten commandments', is presumably the best known to western civilization, and not least in countries which have a Lutheran tradition. In fact Luther incorporated the ten commandments into his *Kleiner Katechismus*, and in the centuries since the Reformation this *Kleiner Katechismus* has had a firmly established position as an instrument of instruction in schools and confirmation classes. As a result of Luther's incomparable explanation of them the commandments have come to be used as an introduction to the true fear of God and Christian living. The form in which he has presented them is *quomodo paterfamilias ea suae familiae simplicissime tradere debeat*. In close connection with his ideas on the earthly calling of Christian men he sets the ten commandments before our eyes as a statement of those works which are good and well-pleasing to God and which a Christian man should put into practice in the ordinary daily 'domestic' life which each one passes with his neighbours. Thus orientated towards the morality of everyday life the ten commandments become, in Luther's hand, a weapon to turn against the veneration of saints, the doctrine of justification by works and the monkish pietism of the Catholic Church.[1]

Whether Luther's uncompromisingly Protestant interpretation of the ten commandments has been able to survive in communities which have been influenced in other ways by the Lutheran tradition is perhaps doubtful. Nevertheless it is fact a that

---

[1] Cf. above all the *Catechismus Major*, I Pars, Conclusio Decalogi. The exegesis of the first commandment as definitive for the rest, and the interpretation of the fear of God as confidence of heart and trust in God are also Protestant characteristics. By adding positive supplements to the prohibitions and negative supplements to the commands Luther has brilliantly re-ordered and unified the ten commandments, giving them as a series a homogeneity which from a formal point of view they do not in themselves possess. Analogies for this are to be found in the Old Testament itself in Lev. 19.9-10, 15, 17 and especially in the well-known passage 19.18.

in the mind of the ordinary man it is rather Luther's explanation of the concrete particulars contained in each individual commandment that predominates. Such a man is not usually aware that the collection of the commandments as a whole, just as much as the closer understanding of each individual commandment, gives rise to a whole host of problems.[2] In the pages which follow I will attempt briefly to indicate the most important problems which arise when we go beyond the popular catechism version of the commandments in order to study them in the original text and on the basis of the historical and critical research of the past two hundred years.

The first problem which presents itself is the problem of the actual number. Different Churches have different methods of enumerating the commandments, and the method which prevails in orthodox Judaism differs not only from that of the Christian Churches but also from that which was maintained in the Judaism of Jesus' time. On this point the divergence of opinion is so strong that one is tempted to doubt whether the number ten as applied to the commandments in Ex. 20 and Deut. 5 has any real authenticity. Moreover an analysis of the contents reveals that the collection as we now have it contains doublets. In this connection we may mention the problem of how the ten commandments should be divided between the two tables. We shall be treating of the problems indicated here in the first chapter of this work.

The next series of problems which presents itself concerns the exact interpretation of the individual words and sentences in the 'ten commandments'. As I see it these problems can be solved only when their investigation is accompanied by an analysis of the literary, form-critical and traditio-historical problems of the decalogue. For this reason I do not propose to undertake any special exegetical examination of the decalogue in a separate section, but will treat of the exegetical problems

[2] As one of the grounds for this assertion we may mention a series of broadcasts by the Danish National Radio in the spring of 1961. In these, personalities of public life (not theologians) discussed the contents of the ten commandments and their meaning for the present day. As a rule it is only the prohibitions of murder and marital infidelity that give rise to exegetical considerations.

throughout the sections as and when the need for this makes itself felt.

A special complex of problems can be grouped under the heading of 'The Literary Problems of the Decalogue'. Here our first problem is to establish the text of the two versions of the decalogue which we have before us in Exodus and Deuteronomy respectively, which seem to have exercised a mutual influence upon each other in the process of transmission (the problem of textual criticism). This problem leads on naturally to the discussion of the next one, namely that of the literary relationship between the two versions of the decalogue. This problem is in turn connected with the question of how each version is related to the context in which it now stands. In view of the developments in Old Testament research since the middle of the last century this latter problem also implies that we must define our position with regard to the 'sources' theory, according to which the Pentateuch must be a conflation of at least four different literary sources.[3] Discussion of this problem leads us still further, for it shows that it is necessary to touch upon the relationship between the 'ten commandments' and such collections as the 'Book of the Covenant[4] and the 'cultic decalogue'.[5] In the

---

[3] In its classic formulation the Reuss-Graf-Kuenen-Wellhausen hypothesis maintains that the Pentateuch is composed of four literary written sources (designated as J=Yahwist, E=Elohist, D=Deuteronomy and P=the Priestly Code). J belongs to the period of the great prophets. E must reflect prophetic influence, which makes itself felt to a still greater extent in D. This in its original form must in its turn have provided the basis for the Josian reform of 622 BC. The latest of these sources is P, which belongs to exilic or post-exilic times. While the *distribution* of the material between the four sources is often based on very acute observations concerning differences of style, the reduplication of episodes and the appearance of contradictions, the conclusions of the critics regarding the *date* and *characterization* of the written sources referred to here rely, to a certain extent, on a basic preconception of how Israelite culture must have developed. A penetrating evaluation both of the methods and of the conception of history of higher criticism has been made by *Johannes Pedersen* (cf. especially his work *Israel* III-IV, ET, 1940, pp. 725ff.), who may be regarded as the 'father' or founder of the Scandinavian branch of the 'traditio-historical school'.

[4] Ex. 20.22-23.33. The name is derived (rightly or wrongly) from Ex. 24.7.

[5] Ex. 34.13-26. The expression 'the ten commandments' is applied to this collection in v. 28. It has been concluded in higher-critical circles that this verse belongs to J and that it is earlier than Ex. 20. Against this in Deut. 4.13 and 10.4 the expression 'the ten commandments' is used of the classic decalogue (Ex. 20= Deut. 5).

second chapter of this treatise we shall be discussing the problems mentioned here.

The researches of form-criticism which have given new and decisive impulses to Old and New Testament studies alike, have, so far as the decalogue is concerned, made us aware of problems the existence of which was less keenly felt at an earlier date. The literary form of the decalogue assigns it to that part of the legal material of the Old Testament which has been called 'apodictic law'.[6] Since apodictic law elsewhere is characterized by individual sentences grouped in either short or long series and displaying the same structure, it is on these grounds remarkable that two of the ten commandments are actually formulated as commands while the rest are presented as prohibitions. A further striking feature so far as the decalogue is concerned is the wide variation in the length of the commandments. The prohibitions regarding the service of idols and coveting the house of a neighbour are extremely full, as too are the commands concerning sabbath observance and honouring parents. By contrast the prohibitions of murder, unfaithfulness and theft are remarkably short. A further decisive factor from a form-critical point of view is the question of the original context of a passage.[7] Did the text originally belong to the instruction which the father of a family would have given to his household?[8] Or is the original context of the passage some religious event such as may be referred to, for instance, in the introduction to the decalogue? We shall be treating of the form-critical problems in Chapter III.

[6] The expression 'apodictic' was first used by Albrecht Alt to express a particular type of Old Testament law. cf. '*Die Ursprünge des israelitischen Rechts*, 1934, ET, 'The Origins of Israelite Law', *Essays on Old Testament History and Religion*, 1966, pp. 81ff. The objective phenomenon to which Alt refers is the separation of the 'secular justice' of the ancient Near East, which was formulated casuistically, from the 'sacral justice', which was expressed in rhythmic form and religiously motivated. Alt was not the first to discover this. Among his predecessors we may mention particularly B. Baentsch: *Das Bundesbuch*, 1892 and Alfred Jepsen: *Untersuchungen zum Bundesbuch*, 1927. The latter is a pupil of Alt and wrote his book under his inspiration, as emerges from his preface. In Aristotelian logic the expression 'apodictic' is used of a logical judgment. It asserts that a given relationship must necessarily be thus and cannot be otherwise, all other possibilities being excluded.

[7] Cf. the apt expression employed by Hermann Gunkel, '*Sitz-im-Leben*'.

[8] Cf. Luther's words quoted above from the *Catechismus Minor*.

The conclusions arising from the problems which we have felt it necessary to discuss in the first three chapters of this treatise will be summed up in the fourth chapter, the history of the transmission (*Überlieferungsgeschichte*) of the decalogue. In this chapter we shall attempt to trace the decalogue from what may be presumed to be its original form to the form in which it exists today in Ex. 20 and Deut. 5. At the same time we shall attempt to determine the forces which have contributed to the modification of the decalogue. It is hoped that at the same time this will have the effect of throwing light upon the cultural, social and religious history through which the Israelites lived on the soil of Canaan.

This brings us to our final series of problems connected with the decalogue: the much discussed questions concerning the 'age' and Mosaic authorship of the decalogue. These questions will be treated of in the fifth chapter, which we intend to round off with a brief glance at the 'history of the influence' of the decalogue.

I

WHY TEN COMMANDMENTS?

1. WHY ARE THERE *ten* COMMANDMENTS?

WHAT is the significance of the number ten for the commandments? Anyone attempting to solve this problem on the basis of an investigation of the use of the number ten throughout the Old Testament finds himself confronted with materials of the most complex and varied nature, materials which, moreover, are chiefly drawn from the narrative and legal sections.[1] We may disregard those occurrences in which the use of the number ten certainly derives from some isolated historical circumstance, e.g. the temporal data in Judg. 12.11; II Kings 15.17; cf. also Gen. 16.3; Ruth 1.4; I Sam. 25.38 and Jer. 42.7; also Josh. 21.5 and 26 (the ten cities of the priestly family of the Kohathites) and Jer. 41.8 (the ten men who escaped the fate of being cut down by Ishmael).

Apart from these there remain the use of the number ten in weights and measures, its function in sacred architecture, in the institution of the tithe, in counting an assembly or groups of persons with particular avocations, and finally the proverbial use of the expression 'ten times'.

Weights and Measures. The number ten has a definite function in the system of dry measure: 1 *'ēpā* = 10 *'ōmer* (Ex. 16.36) and 1 *ḥōmer* = 10 *'ēpā* (Ezek. 45.11). *'ēpā* and *ḥōmer* are loan-words deriving from the Egyptian *'ipt* and the Akkadian *imēru*. What precise meaning these definitions of measure bore in the pre-exilic period of Israel cannot be decided. According to their etymology *ḥōmer* must mean a normal ass's load, and *'ōmer* a sheaf of corn. The above mentioned systematization based on

---

[1] The survey which follows makes no claim to be comprehensive.

units of ten must have derived from the functionaries at the Israelite sanctuaries, for the term *'iśśarōn*, 'a tenth' (i.e. a tenth of an *'ēpā*) occurs chiefly in the cultic legislation (Ex. 29. 40; Lev. 14.10; Num. 28.5 and elsewhere).[2] In Ezek. 45.11-14 the system for measuring fluids is brought into correlation with that described above: 1 *kōr* = 10 *bat*, and *kōr* = *ḥōmer*, *bat* = *'ēpā*. In the same passage the 'decimal' system is extended to weights and coinage: 1 *mānē* = 50 *šeqel*, 1 *šeqel* = 20 *gērā*.

It appears probable that this method of dividing into units of ten is related to the institution of the tithe. There are numerous indications that this form of sacred gift or 'tax' was introduced with the advent of the monarchy. At the two royal sanctuaries, Bethel in the northern kingdom (Amos 4.4) and Jerusalem in the southern (Deut. 12.17; 14.22; Mal. 3.8, 10; Neh. 10.36ff.) the prescribed harvest offering took the form of the tithe, and in the condemnation of the monarchy ascribed to Samuel in I Sam. 8.11-18 it is asserted (vv. 15 and 17) that the king will take tithes from the corn and wine harvests of the Israelites as well as from their flocks. In complete harmony with this is the fact that in both the passages in Genesis where the tithe is mentioned it is associated with Salem (Jerusalem, Gen. 14.20) and Bethel (Gen. 28.22). However this by no means implies that the number ten must have borne a special symbolic or religious character. The decimal system is and remains for all periods the handiest (in the truest sense of the word) method of counting.[3]

However, the fact that the number ten did have some kind of religious meaning is to be deduced from the three explicit descriptions of sanctuaries which we have in the Old Testament, namely Ex. 25ff., I Kings 6ff. and Ezek. 40ff. Here let us confine ourselves to the description of the furnishings of Solomon's temple, I Kings 6ff., an account the accuracy of which there is no reason to doubt. In the holy of holies, which was cubic in shape, being twenty cubits in length, breadth and height (6.20),

---

[2] A fuller discussion, with reference to the system of weights and measures employed by Israel's neighbours, is to be found in R. de Vaux, *Ancient Israel*, ET, 1961, pp. 199-206.

[3] Cf. the Greek verb to count (on the fingers), πεμπάζεσθαι (*Odyssey* IV, 412).

stood the two cherubim, each with a wing-span of ten cubits.
These were so placed that the outer wing-tips of each touched
one of the walls, while their inner wing-tips met and touched
each other at the centre. In the main court of the temple there
stood, in addition to the altar of incense and the table for the
shewbread, ten lamps, five on the right side as one faced the
holy of holies, and five on the left (7.49). In the space before
the temple structure were the ten stands with the ten lavers of
bronze, five on the south side and five on the north (7.27-39).[4]
Probably the precise religious symbolism associated with the
number ten cannot be determined. It must be said, however,
that behind the erection of the Jerusalem temple stood the
tradition of Phoenician architecture,[5] and that from the pre-
monarchical traditions of Israelite history one would rather
have expected twelve lamps and twelve lavers, six on either
side, cf. e.g. Deut. 27. In connection with our subject it is interesting to notice the arrangement of these collections of ten
objects in two equal groups. This imparts a certain probability
to the attempt to divide the ten commandments between the
two tables of the law with five on each table.[6]

[4] Benzinger, *Die Bücher der Könige*, 1899, p. 55, and Montgomery and Gehman,
The Books of Kings, 1951, p. 183, regard the pericope on the lamps as secondary
and devoid of historical value. Mowinckel, *De tidligere Profeter* ('The Former
Prophets'), 1935, pp. 326ff. likewise considers these verses secondary, but believes
that the information concerning the lamps *could* derive from an ancient tradition.

[5] A fact which is expressly brought to our attention in I Kings 5.32 and 7.40ff.,
and which is further emphasized by the fact that Solomon's temple is closely related in type to the temple of *tell Tainat* in northern Syria of the eighth century BC;
cf. e.g. G. E. Wright, *BA* 4.2, 1941, pp. 17ff. In the summer of 1963, in the course
of the excavation of *tell 'Arad* in southern Palestine, Israeli archeologists un-
covered part of an Israelite sanctuary with three divisions, similar in type to the
one mentioned above and going back to the period of Solomon. For a preliminary
notice by the archeologist in charge of the excavation see Y. Aharoni in *RB* 20,
1964, pp. 393-396.

[6] With reference to the view that the Deuteronomists are responsible for the
present form of the Books of Kings, the Deuteronomist tradition to the effect that
both tables with the ten commandments upon them were put into 'the ark of the
covenant' (Deut. 10.1-5) might be adduced in the present context with a certain
degree of probability. In the account of the consecration of Solomon's temple,
I Kings 8, it is striking how much emphasis is laid upon the fact that the ark contained just these two stone tables, representing the sealing of the covenant, and
nothing else, v. 9. However the question is considerably more complex, see below,
pp. 30-34.

A few examples exist of the way the numeral ten was used in *the enumeration of those engaged in the same employment*. In Lev. 26.26 this usage is primarily proverbial: ten women shall bake bread in a single oven. (For a parallel to this cf. Isa. 4.1: seven women shall take hold of one man.) Again in II Sam. 15.16 (20.3) when David fled from Absalom he left ten concubines behind at Jerusalem to keep his house. More significantly, mention is frequently made of patrols of ten men as the smallest military unit (I Sam. 25.5; II Sam. 18.15; II Kings 25.25; Jer. 41.1; cf. also Ex. 18.21). The same practical considerations which we have already supposed to lie behind the system of counting by tens (see above) appear to have been decisive in this context also.[7]

In conclusion we must again draw attention to the *proverbial* use of the expression 'ten times' as a device of intensification (Gen. 31.7, 41; Num. 14.22; Neh. 4.12; Job 19.3; Dan. 1.20). In this connection it must also be mentioned that what we call 'decimation' as applied to troops in battle is explicitly referred to by Amos (Amos 5.3; 6.9; cf. also Judg. 20.10).

The results of this survey may seem meagre. Traces are to be found in the Old Testament of the fact that the numeral ten, as applied to the temple at Jerusalem, had a symbolic or religious significance in the period of the monarchy. But we cannot determine what that significance was. Again it may be supposed that the numeral ten played an important part in military and administrative affairs for the reason that a man's ten fingers constitute a readily available starting-point for any kind of enumeration. As an analogy for the division of the ten commandments between the two tables we have been able to adduce an example from Solomon's temple, namely the arrangement of the lamps and bronze lavers, together with the equipment that went with them, into two groups. The modesty of this

[7] In Ex. 18.21 the military method of dividing troops is transferred to the context of the administration of justice in civil life. It is possible that the summoning of precisely ten of the elders of Bethlehem to try a case (Ruth 4.2) is to be understood in the light of some such method of organization. Subsequently the unit of ten had a remarkable importance in later Judaism, for students of the law were organized in groups of ten. This practice was followed notably by the Pharisees and the Essenes (for the latter cf. Josephus, *Bellum* II, 146, and further, in the Qumran writings 1QS VI, 3ff., 1QSa II, 22).

conclusion may be compared with the ingenious speculations concerning the significance of the numeral ten put forward by the Alexandrian Jew Philo in his *De decalogo*.[8]

2. THE TRADITIONAL ENUMERATIONS

One of the minor practical difficulties encountered in the study of the scholarly literature on the decalogue is the fact that three different methods of enumerating the ten commandments are presupposed. In his *Kleiner Katechismus* Luther follows the enumeration of the Roman Catholic Church as established by Augustine. Calvin and the Reformed Church which follows him has an enumeration which can claim support from both Josephus and Philo (i.e. from the Judaism of the period of Jesus) and which in fact possesses certain advantages over the Catholic and Lutheran enumerations. Orthodox Judaism counts the introduction to the decalogue as a separate commandment and in this respect deviates a little from the enumeration of the Reformed Church. All this may be set out schematically as follows:

Ex. 20	Josephus Philo	Catholic Lutheran	Reformed	Jewish	Content
v. 2				I	Introduction
v. 3	I	I	I	II	Against polytheism
v. 4	II	(I)	II	II	Against image worship
vv. 5-6 v. 7	III	II	III	III	Against misuse of God's name
vv. 8-11	IV	III	IV	IV	The sabbath
v. 12	V	IV	V	V	Parents
v. 13	VI/VII	V	VI	VI	Against murder
v. 14	VII/VI	VI	VII	VII	Against adultery
v. 15	VIII	VII	VIII	VIII	Against theft
v. 16	IX	VIII	IX	IX	Against false witness
v. 17	X	IX-X	X	X	Against covetousness

[8] Cf. *De decalogo* 20: ten is the perfect number which contains all kinds of numbers, even and odd alike, and also the 'even odd'; *ib.*, 23: the term 'decade' derives from the fact that the numeral ten can take in (δέχεσθαι) all numerals. Ten is the sum of the categories etc.

The Lutheran enumeration differs from that of Augustine in two respects. First it omits the prohibition of image worship, which Augustine puts with the first commandment, secondly it gives the ninth commandment as 'Thou shalt not covet thy neighbour's house', while Augustine takes the text from Deut. 5.21a: 'Neither shall you covet your neighbour's wife.' Again in Philo's version the prohibition of adultery is placed before that of murder. In this sense there are in reality five different methods of enumeration in existence.

Measured against the actual form of the decalogue as we have it in Ex. 20 and Deut. 5 (the variations between these two versions are for our present purpose irrelevant) none of these methods of enumeration escapes criticism. Neither in its form nor in its content is Ex. 20.2 a commandment. In this respect Orthodox Judaism, which regards it as the first commandment, is open to criticism. Then in order to maintain the number of commandments as ten Orthodox Judaism has conflated the prohibition of the worship of other gods with the prohibition of image worship so as to form a single commandment despite the fact that the sense of Ex. 20.3 and 20.4 appears to demand that they shall be taken as two distinct commandments. Augustine has done the same except that he has taken vv. 3-4 as the first commandment. Luther has simply omitted the prohibition of images. In this he has merely followed the general practice of the Roman Catholic Church from the thirteenth century onwards.[1] At first glance, and if one confines one's vision to Ex. 20.3-4, it seems that Josephus, Philo and the Reformed Church have carried out the only correct method of enumeration. But as soon as one extends one's vision so as to include vv. 5-6 the reasoning of Orthodox Judaism, as well as that of the Catholic

[1] A comprehensive account of the extremely varied history of the prohibition of images and the decisive reasons for its omission from the Catholic catechism from the early Middle Ages onwards is provided by R. H. Charles in *The Decalogue*, 1923, pp. 14-88, cf. especially pp. 68ff. In the Eastern Church, where the veneration of images has in fact predominated from early times, its complete legality being upheld by the highest authority in the Eastern Church, John Damascene (eighth century), the prohibition of images has been maintained. But it has been held to apply to images carved out of stone, so that painted wooden images have not been affected.

and Lutheran Churches becomes at least comprehensible. For vv. 5-6 are syntactically linked with v. 3 in such a way that together with it they form a frame round the prohibition of images in v. 4, making it a subdivision of the commandment not to have other gods. In other words on these grounds it is not so arbitrary to take vv. 3-6 as a single commandment. A more manifest defect in the Catholic and Lutheran methods of enumeration is the division of v. 17 (the prohibition of covetousness) into two commandments. It is true that formally speaking this division can be justified, for both the negation and the verb in 17a are repeated in 17b.[2] But for this approach to be consistently followed through vv. 4-6 would also have to be divided into three commandments, and the same course would have to be taken with vv. 8-11.[3] As to the divergence between Josephus and Philo, namely whether the prohibition of killing should be placed before or after that of adultery,[4] it is difficult to arrive at an objective conclusion on this point. Both crimes were considered, from early times, as liable to the death penalty (Ex. 21.12; Lev. 20.10).

None of the traditional attempts to divide the text in its existing form into ten commandments is wholly above criticism. Most of the difficulties arising in connection with the actual number ten can be solved by applying historical or form-critical principles.[5] Yet it can cause no surprise that it has sometimes been called in question whether Ex. 20 and Deut. 5 really were

[2] In the version of Deuteronomy the verb *ḥāmad* is replaced by the verb *hit'awwe* for the sake of variation. In this respect, as in almost all others, the Deuteronomist form is secondary by comparison with that of Exodus, see below, p. 43.

[3] On this see the attempted reconstruction of the decalogue by Hans Schmidt in *Eucharisterion*, 1923, pp. 78-119, 'Mose und der Dekalog'. The Sabbath commandment and the commandment to honour parents are first cut out because of their positive formulation, and then vv. 3-7, are divided into 5 commandments: (1) Thou shalt have no other gods before me; (2) thou shalt not bow down thyself unto them; (3) thou shalt not serve them; (4) thou shalt not make unto thee a graven image; (5) thou shalt not take the name 'Yahweh' in vain. This proposed reconstruction has found no support elsewhere. Further on this cf. pp. 78ff. below.

[4] Josephus and Philo really represent the Palestinian and Egyptian traditions respectively on this point. Mark 10.19 (Matt. 19.18), like LXX cod. AF on Ex. 20.13f. and Deut, 5.17, reflect the Palestinian tradition, while LXX cod. B, the Nash papyrus and Luke 18.20 represent the Egyptian.

[5] See below, pp. 78-86.

intended as a decalogue.[6] However against this it must be remembered that as early as the sixth century BC (cf. Deut. 4.13 and 10.4) the passage under consideration was regarded as a collection of 'ten words'.[7] Even so it would naturally have been more satisfactory if this way of taking Deut. 4 and 10 could have been supported by analogous usages.

3. ANALOGIES FROM THE PENTATEUCH AND ELSEWHERE

The attempt to discover other decalogues in the Old Testament was initiated by Goethe in a short essay written in letter form, 'Zwo wichtige, bisher unerörterte biblische Fragen, zum erstenmal gründlich beantwortet', *Von einem Landgeistlichen in Schwaben*, 1773.[1] The 'first question' put forward in this monograph is 'What was written on the tables of the covenant?' To answer it he adduces Ex. 34.14-26, a passage which according to his interpretation contains ten commandments, that is, four

---

[6] Cf. Erhard Gerstenberger, *Wesen und Herkunft des sogenannten apodiktischen Rechts in Alten Testament*, 1961, pp. 77ff., and most recently Henning Graf Reventlow, *Gebot und Predigt im Dekalog*, 1962, pp. 12ff.: 'The numeral ten is an artificial factor and has sometimes led to a somewhat forced arrangement of the text into precisely ten commandments. Either the exact number ten has been selected more or less arbitrarily from a longer section of text, or a shorter amount has been extended, again forcibly, so as to make up the required number.' Presumably Reventlow intends this criticism to apply to the various efforts which have been made to find decalogues in other passages of the Old Testament apart from Ex. 20 and Deut. 5. As a curious illustration of what he is referring to we may adduce the attempted reconstruction published in 1846 by Ernst Meier, the Tübingen Orientalist, under the title *Die ursprüngliche Form des Dekalogs*. The introductory words of the decalogue are taken as the first commandment. Following on from this the second to the fifth commandment comprise the prohibitions of polytheism, image worship, and the misuse of the divine name and also the sabbath commandment, all in the shortest form possible. The sixth to the tenth commandments, ascribed to the second table, comprise the command to honour parents, and the prohibitions of adultery, murder, false witness and theft. The prohibition of covetousness is considered as a 'doublet' or 'further extension' of the prohibition of stealing. On this last point Meier anticipates Johannes Herrmann in 'Das zehnte Gebot', *Festschrift für Sellin*, 1927, pp. 69-82. Less convincing is Meier's ingenious attempt to establish an underlying connection between the first and sixth commandments, the second and seventh, the third and eighth, etc. See further on, pp. 78f.

[7] On the actual Hebrew expression '*aseret hadd^ebārīm*, and on the use of *debar-Yahweh* of legal decrees cf. Oskar Grether, *Name und Wort Gottes im Alten Testament*, 1934, pp. 79-83. Further on this cf. below, pp. 49f.

[1] Cited from *Goethes Werke. Auswahl in 16 Bänden*, Leipzig (Reclams Ausgabe), 1910, Vol. 7, pp. 146-152.

prohibitions and six positive commands: 1) You shall worship
no other god. 2) The feast of unleavened bread you shall keep.
3) All that opens the womb is mine; and all your male cattle,
the firstlings of cow and sheep. 4) Six days you shall work, but
on the seventh day you shall rest; in ploughing time and in
harvest you shall rest. 5) You shall observe the feast of weeks,
the first fruits of wheat harvest, and the feast of ingathering at
the year's end. 6) Three times in the year shall all your males
appear before the Lord Your God. 7) You shall not offer the
blood of my sacrifice with leaven. 8) Neither shall the sacrifice
of the feast of passover be left until the morning. 9) The first of
the first fruits of your ground you shall bring to the house of the
Lord your God. 10) You shall not boil a kid when it is still dependent upon its mother's milk. On the basis of Ex. 34.28 Goethe
maintains that these are the ten commandments that are a witness
to the covenant made by the Lord with Israel exclusively, and that
it was these commandments that he imposed upon her. Hence it
was not the 'most universal truths' expressed in the classic decalogue that formed the basis of the covenant between God and
Israel. Now a covenant which is, of its nature, confined to one
particular people can hardly have 'universal binding force'. The
Jewish people ('a wild and barren stock') first attained true
universality when the eternal gardener grafted onto that stock
the noble shoot that is Jesus Christ.

A hundred years later Julius Wellhausen 'rediscovered' the
'cultic decalogue' in Ex. 34.[2] He argued for a similar kind of

---

[2] *Die Composition des Hexateuchs und der historischen Bücher des alten Testaments*, 2nd
impr., 1889, pp. 86ff., and above all 'Nachträge', pp. 327ff., where Wellhausen
(p. 328, n. 1) draws attention to the fact that he had independently arrived at the
same conclusion as Goethe, and that Goethe's essay, mentioned above, was first
brought to his attention by one of his students after he had completed his own
interpretation. According to Wellhausen the earliest or 'Yahwist' decalogue in
Ex. 34 has in its present form been worked over by editors so that it now appears
as a 'dodecalogue' (i.e. a collection of 12 commandments). However it can be
reduced to a decalogue first by cutting out the sabbath commandment, which
occurs as an interpolation between the laws relating to the annual festivals, and
second by removing the commandment concerning the three yearly pilgrimages,
which, by reason of each one receiving a separate mention, gives an impression of
superfluity; cf. pp. 331ff. Both in *Die Composition* . . . and in the *Prolegomena to the
History of Israel*, ET, 1885, reprinted 1962, p. 83, Wellhausen applies the description 'Law of the Two Tables' (*Zweitafelgesetz*) to Ex. 34.14ff.

opposition between the classic decalogue of Ex. 20 and this ritual decalogue of Ex. 34, in that he characterized the relationship between the two as the same as that between Amos and his contemporaries (i.e. as the opposition between the prophetic and the popular attitudes).[3]

Wellhausen's authority was one of the chief factors which caused the idea of a decalogue in Ex. 34 to win general acceptance among Old Testament scholars, although all through the relevant period, and even from the side of higher criticism, objections to the theory were being raised, among other reasons because the number ten could be arrived at only by considerably reducing the text of Ex. 34. Today one senses a growing scepticism with regard to the theory.[4]

In several passages of the Pentateuch we encounter series of commands, prohibitions and curses which are similar in form, and in the majority of these cases attempts have at some time been made to show that the series concerned contains the number ten. As the first instance of such a series we may mention Deut. 27.15-16, a collection of twelve curses which therefore constitute, in their present form, a dodecalogue. This dode-

---

[3] *Die Composition* . . . , p. 87, n. 2. According to him the decalogue in Ex. 20 represents, by comparison with that of Ex. 34, 'an extremely significant advance'.

[4] Wellhausen's reconstruction in the 'Nachträgen' (see above, p. 14, n. 2) is, as he himself attests, at variance with his first attempt in *Die Composition* . . . , p. 87, n. 2. Mowinckel gives a survey of previous attempts at a reconstruction in his book *Le Décalogue*, 1927, pp. 19ff. He prefers to reduce the thirteen commandments which he finds in Ex. 34.14-26 by taking these relating to the three principal festivals as subsequent—and correct—additions making the commandment concerning pilgrimages more precise, *op. cit.*, 22ff. C. Cornill, together with numerous other disciples of Wellhausen, shows himself decisively in favour of the theory of the cultic decalogue. Cf. *Einleitung in die kanonischen Bücher des Alten Testaments*, 7th ed., 1913, p. 44. Among the more recent adherents of this theory we may mention R. H. Pfeiffer, *Introduction to the Old Testament*, 1941, pp. 221ff., and A. Lods, *Histoire de la littérature hébraïque et juive*, 1950, pp. 201ff. S. R. Driver maintains a hesitant attitude in *An Introduction to the Literature of the Old Testament*, 1892, pp. 36ff. Kuenen shows himself sceptical towards the idea of a decalogue in Ex. 34 (cf. Wellhausen, *Die Composition* . . . p. 328), while Dillmann, in *Die Bücher Exodus und Leviticus*, 2nd ed., 1880, p. 352, rejects it completely. Steuernagel, in *Lehrbuch der Einleitung in Das Alte Testament*, 1912, p. 155, and Baudissin, *Einleitung in die Bücher des Alten Testaments*, 1901, pp. 130ff. likewise reject the theory. Among the more recent opponents of this theory of a cultic decalogue it must suffice to mention Albrecht Alt, 'Origins of Israelite Law', p. 117, n. 95; Walther Zimmerli, *The Law and the Prophets*, ET, Oxford, 1965, New York, 1967, p. 33, and especially Hans Kosmala, 'The So-called Ritual Decalogue', *ASTI* 1, 1962, pp. 31-61.

calogue of curses is used in the course of a ceremony of covenant ratification, and as part of a ritual performed by the chosen leader of the Israelite twelve-tribe confederation with the Levitical priests as his assistants. This context underlines the fact that the characteristic setting in which commandments are proclaimed is one of ritual and ceremony. Of all the collections of laws in the Old Testament this dodecalogue of curses is the one of which, from its present literary context, we can most clearly define the original context, that is the context in which it would once have been proclaimed. Yet even this is true only to a limited extent, for naturally it is always possible that the dodecalogue has been set in its present position quite deliberately in order to suggest an original context different from the one in which it did in fact emerge.

If we take this possibility into account we shall also keep open minds on the question of whether the text of Deut. 27.15ff. has been expanded by secondary additions. This might have been done in order to extend a somewhat shorter series into a series of 'twelve words' corresponding to the twelve tribes, who give their assent to the collection as a whole by saying 'Amen' to each law.[5] In other words the question can be raised whether this series originally constituted a decalogue.

Now concerning the 'originality' of the twelve curses doubts have been expressed on exegetical grounds. Whereas the rest of the eleven curses are concerned with quite concrete actions (e.g. image worship, oppression of the sojourner, the fatherless and the widow in legal causes, incest and homicide), v. 26 runs, in a style which is typically Deuteronomist: 'Cursed be he who does not confirm the words of this law by doing them.'[6]

[5] I have offered an exegetical and traditio-historical treatment of Deut. 27 in *Shechem. A Traditio-historical Investigation*, 1955, pp. 50-85. The division of (the representatives of) the twelve tribes into two groups standing opposite one another is, of course, to be explained from the place where the ceremony took place, between Ebal and Gerizim.

[6] The use of *heqîm*, 'confirm', is less typically Deuteronomist, although it is found in Deut. 8.18 and 9.5 with Yahweh as subject. On the other hand the expressions *dibrē hattōrā hazzōt*, 'the words of this law' (Deut. 17.19; 27.3, 8; 28.58; 29.28; 31.12, 24; 32.46) and *la'asōt* 'and perform' (Deut. *passim* of carrying out the law) are markedly Deuteronomist.

Arguments have also been adduced against the originality of the first of these twelve commandments, with regard to both form and content. While the commandments from the second to the eleventh are identical in construction, *'ārūr* + participle with object or prepositional connection, v. 15 is formulated as follows: *'ārūr hā'îš 'ªšer ya'ªse* etc., i.e. predicate + relative clause.[7] Moreover it is the only one of the concrete curses which is directed against a cultic crime. The fact that the polemic against image worship is a major preoccupation of the Deuteronomists (cf. Deut. 4.15ff., 25; 7.4ff.; 9.7ff.) could explain why they were particularly interested in adding on this commandment, and in setting it first in the series.[8]

Lev. 18.6-17 is a passage which raises problems similar to those which we have encountered in the collection in Deut. 27.15ff. It consists of a series of prohibitions directed against sexual relations within the extended family, i.e. with other members of the family of one's own generation, of the generation preceding and of the generations of the children and the children's children.[9] The existing text contains a series of eleven prohibitions constructed on a pattern expressed in the formula

[7] It is of course possible to reconstruct a primitive form of this commandment approximately as follows: *'ārūr sām pesel bassᵉtār.* cf. Alt, 'Origins . . .', p. 115, n. 86. The secondary formulation could in that case be regarded as expressing the emphasis which was laid upon this commandment at a later date. But if we still wanted to reconstruct a decalogue we would have to omit one of the following curses and merely as a hypothesis we might propose v. 21 (against sodomy), which is placed in the midst of a group of curses for incest (cf. also Minette de Tillese in *VT* 12, 1962, p. 77).

[8] According to the sound form-critical approach which characterizes Albrecht Alt's work on 'The Origins of Israelite law', the loosening of the style must be regarded as a sign of the diminished ability of writers of later periods to keep the various types distinct from each other (the laws of Deuteronomy themselves are a sufficient example). On these grounds the first and the twelfth commandments of the dodecalogue of curses must, all things considered, be the ones which most of all give rise to exegetical speculations. Mowinckel's opposition to Alt's fundamental standpoint is expressed in his article 'Zur Geschichte der Dekaloge', *ZAW* 55, 1937, pp. 219ff., n. 1. He would severely restrict the possibility of arriving at conclusions on questions of date on the basis of form-critical research. In his research on the psalms one is not aware in Mowinckel of any trace of this attitude to form-criticism. The most recent research follows in its general lines the basic approach of Alt. An exception is Henning Graf Reventlow, cf. e.g. his *Gebot und Predigt im Dekalog*, 1962, p. 80.

[9] It might perhaps be suggested that this idea of the extended family is reflected in the familiar formula 'to the third and the fourth generation' as found in the

'*erwat NN lō' tᵉgallē*, 'Thou shalt not uncover the nakedness of NN'. Karl Elliger[10] has shown on good grounds that by a simple scribal error one sentence has been omitted from the collection as it now exists, namely the prohibition of uncovering the nakedness of the daughter (between v. 9 and v. 10). At some period therefore the text must have appeared as a dodecalogue. But on Elliger's view two of the prohibitions cannot have been included in the original series, namely that referring to the mother's sister in v. 18—in the context of the patriarchal community she does not belong to the extended family—and v. 17, which treats of relations with both mother and daughter. This verse differs from the previous ones in that it has two objects. Thus what has come to be a dodecalogue is reduced to a decalogue, which Elliger, working from the basis of his general theory of the extended family, assigns to the nomadic period of Israel, that is to the period before Moses.[11] The numerous accretions which the text in its present form contains, and which can be shown to be accretions by form-critical methods,[12] have modified Lev. 18.6ff. for proclamation in a cultic setting reminiscent of that which we have encountered in Deut. 27. It is community instruction intended to establish that state of holiness which the community of Yahweh must achieve in order to encounter Yahweh himself in the cult.[13] The apodictic formulation of the clauses of the original decalogue may well be due to the influence of Yahweh religion.

classic decalogue and elsewhere (Ex. 20.5; Deut. 5.9; cf. also Ex. 34.7 and Num. 14.18). According to S. Segert, '"Bis in das dritte und vierte Glied" (Ex. 20.5)'. *Communio Viatorum* 1, 1958, pp. 37-39, here cited from *ZAW* 71, 1959, p. 218, the Beduin confine blood feuds to the four most proximate degrees of relationship.

[10] 'Das Gesetz Leviticus 18', *ZAW* 67, 1955, pp. 1-25.

[11] The objection might be raised that the narrator of Gen. 20 has let Abraham the nomad be married to his half-sister. Elliger believes (*op. cit.*, p. 7) that the prohibition of cohabitation with a sister was originally directed only against such cohabitation with a full sister.

[12] This applies both to expansions within the individual legal maxims (as for example the motivating clauses vv. 7a, 7b, 8b, 9b, 10b, etc.) and to the total framework within which we now find the original law contained, as vv. 1-5, the collection of laws in vv. 19ff., and the conclusion, i.e. vv. 24ff.

[13] Cf. Mowinckel's treatment of Pss. 15 and 24 and the discovery of the literary category 'entrance tora', a discovery whose implications are seen in numerous ways in modern form-critical research on the legal material of the Old Testament (Galling, von Rad, Zimmerli, etc.).

But as rules of conduct for the extended family (or better, for the head of the extended family) this decalogue must have originally been a *Haustafel*, containing instruction for the family circle.[14]

Lev. 20.2ff. contains a series of thirteen legal sayings which are, for the most part, constructed after the following pattern: *'iš 'ašer* (+verb), *mōt yūmāt*, 'The man who . . . , shall be put to death.' In form the first of these legal sayings (vv. 2-5) deviates from the rest, both because of its length and also because of its introductory formula, *'iš 'iš*. The next in the series, v. 6 also has a special form of introduction, *hannepeš 'ašer*, 'The person who . . .'. Moreover the penalty is not expressed by the formula *mōt yūmāt*. The third commandment of this series (v. 9) differs from those which follow only by its introductory *'iš 'iš*. The above-mentioned pattern appears most clearly in the fourth to the seventh commandment (vv. 10, 11, 12, 13) and the ninth (v. 15), but even here the singular form *mōt yūmāt* is replaced by the plural in vv. 11-13. In the tenth to the thirteenth commandments (vv. 17, 18, 20, 21) the introductory formula is the one mentioned above, *'iš 'ašer*, but the penalty is expressed in different words: 'They shall be cut off', *nikrᵉtū* (vv. 17-18), 'They shall die childless', *'arīrīm yāmūtū* (v. 20), 'They shall remain childless', *'arīrīm yīhyū* (v. 21). With regard to content the first commandment treats of child sacrifice, the second of soothsaying by conjuring up the spirits of the dead, the third of cursing one's parents; the fourth to the thirteenth are prohibitions of sexual crimes (adultery, incest, sodomy, intercourse with a menstruating woman). In its present form the series is interrupted, first by the exhortation to holiness and obedience to the law in vv. 7-8, secondly by a prohibition of female sodomy in v. 16 and thirdly by the prohibition of sexual relationships with a mother's sister in v. 19, which is all but

[14] By its form designed precisely for the father of the family, a fact which could raise the question of how such *Haustafeln* were handed down in an assembly in which the fathers of families were represented by others. However we can probably gather from the story of Amnon and Tamar in II Sam. 13.12 that the individual members of the family were also familiar with the rules. Tamar refuses to yield to Amnon's desire and thus shows what one can and cannot do in 'Israel'. On this point cf. especially M. Noth, *Das System der zwölf Stämme Israels*, 1930, p. 104.

verbally identical with 18.13. All attempts at reconstructing a decalogue from the foregoing material must remain hypothetical, but criteria both in respect of form and content can be shown to be in harmony. The first three commandments are distinguished from the remaining ten by their introductory formulae, those ten all being concerned with sexual crimes. If the present text of Lev. 20 has as its basis a 'sexual decalogue' then this decalogue, with its lack of clear plan, must reflect a later stage of development by comparison with Lev. 18. The present expanded collection of fifteen commandments in all (of which three differ markedly from the rest in their formulation) comprise protests which are similar in content to the prophetic and Deuteronomist polemic against heathen customs of the late Assyrian period (740 BC onwards).[15]

Lev. 18 and Lev. 20 both belong to the larger complex of laws known to Old Testament research as the Holiness Code,[16] Lev. 17-26. Attempts have also been made to find a decalogue in ch. 19, the chapter in which the well-known commandment to love one's neighbour occurs. Here Mowinckel's attempt[17] is chiefly noteworthy. His starting-point is a distinction drawn between the commandments which are plural and those which are singular in form in the pericope 19.2-18.[18] The decalogue

[15] Child sacrifice, Deut. 18.10; II Kings 23.10; Micah 6.7; Jer. 7.31; Ezek. 16.20; soothsaying by conjuring up the spirits of the dead, Deut. 18.10ff.; Isa. 8.19; 19.3; II Kings 21.6.

[16] This designation derives from August Klostermann's 'Beiträge zur Entstehungsgeschichte des Pentateuchs', *Zeitschrift für lutherische Theologie und Kirche*, 38, 1877, pp. 401-445, reprinted in *Der Pentateuch* I, 1893, pp. 368ff. As works of recent times we must mention Henning Graf Reventlow's *Das Heiligkeitsgesetz*, 1961, and Chr. Feucht's *Untersuchungen zum Heiligkeitsgesetz*, 1964 (published posthumously).

[17] 'Zur Geschichte der Dekaloge', *ZAW* 55, 1937, pp. 218-235.

[18] As is well known the same criterion has played a very significant part in the analysis of Deuteronomy, with regard both to the framework of the Code and to the Code itself. According to Joachim Begrich's interpretation (*Die priesterliche Thora*, 1936, pp. 63-88) commandments and prohibitions formulated in the second person plural (i.e. directed to the assembled laity) are especially characteristic of the priestly instruction of the laity and, in respect of their content, are designed above all to teach the community how to distinguish between clean and unclean, holy and profane. See especially p. 73 and n. 5, where Lev. 19.5-8 is explicitly mentioned. Begrich's extremely sharp demarcation of the Priestly tora (basically it is concerned with the distinction between clean and unclean; the tora has nothing to do with 'justice and morality as such', p. 72, n. 1) relies upon the implicit

in the plural form—Mowinckel calls it Decalogue A—is shown on analysis to comprise vv. 3a + b, 4a + b, the first to the fourth commandments: honouring parents, observing the sabbath, prohibition of idolatry and image worship. The fifth commandment is to be reconstructed from vv. 5-8, in which only the words '*ad yōm haššᵉlīšī*, 'until the third day', have been retained from the supposed original text—the subject is a prohibition of leaving over any of the meat of festal sacrifices until the third day. The sixth commandment directs that in the corn and grape harvests a little should be left in the field or vineyard for the poor and the sojourner, vv. 9-10. Only the opening words, however, have been kept in the plural—this plural form could even be regarded as an attempt to compensate for what has been omitted—and besides this the unusually complex formulation of the commandment is striking.[19] 19. 11a, b, c, 12a contain four very briefly formulated commands in the plural. According to Mowinckel they constitute the seventh to the tenth commandments in the collection (prohibitions of theft, lying, fraud and perjury). We shall be returning to this text in another connection.[20] It is not a decalogue now and it is hard to believe that it ever has been, but it does quite clearly presuppose the present formulation of the 'classic' decalogue, and it is not altogether an accident that the 'prohibitions under penalty of death' (of murder and adultery) are missing from it.[21]

Mowinckel's Decalogue B, in which the precepts are formulated in the singular, extends from v. 13 to v. 17. In v. 13 he finds three commandments (against oppression, robbery

presupposition that cult and ethics were originally quite separate entities, and upon the explicit presupposition (*op. cit.*, p. 73) that the prophets, by using the style of the priestly tora, were the first to introduce material that was ethical in the true sense into this category. Unfortunately Begrich supplies no explanation of Lev. 19.2-4 or of vv. 11-12, which for the most part represent purely ethical instruction. And his attempt to explain the parallelism between *tōrātᵉkā*, 'thy tora' and *mispātᵉkā*, 'thy ordinances' in the ancient blessing of the priestly tribe, Deut. 33.10 (*op. cit.*, p. 64 and p. 67, n. 8) rather gives the impression of special pleading.

[19] In reality it consists of three prohibitions and a command.

[20] See below pp. 110f. and 142f.

[21] If we suppose that the category of Wisdom literature has had an influence on Lev. 19, then the omission of these two commandments becomes understandable. For transgression of them would, from a juridical point of view, be a crime quite different in degree from transgressions of the other precepts recorded in Lev. 19.

and the withholding wages from day-labourers), while v. 14 contains only one (against cursing the deaf and putting stones in the way of the blind). Mowinckel finds the fifth to the seventh commandments in vv. 15-16: against partiality in judgment, talebearing and persecution. And he finds the eighth and ninth commandments in v. 17: against hatred and in favour of judicial decisions in cases which could lead to strife. Finally he finds the tenth commandment in v. 18: 'Thou shalt not maintain a revengeful attitude towards thy fellow countrymen or harbour grudges.' To this is appended a supplement which is expressed in the positive form: 'Thou shalt love thy neighbour as thyself.' Against Mowinckel's attempt to set this 'decalogue' as an integral element in a broader context, and against his proposed dating of it, it can be objected that, following the custom of the thirties, he relies upon a connection between the various collections of laws and the (hypothetical) traditional written sources as envisaged in source criticism, a connection which is today regarded with greater scepticism than ever.[22] But above all it must be said that all this—including his attempt to distinguish a Decalogue B—seems to be carried out quite arbitrarily and runs counter to the elementary principles of form-criticism. As I see it Albrecht Alt comes nearer to the truth when he says of Lev. 19[23] that it is an offshoot of the decalogue that is found here.

Of far greater interest is the parallel to the decalogues of the Pentateuch which Mowinckel has discovered in a context that is clearly cultic, namely Ps. 15.[24] The significance of this for him

[22] Without questioning the validity of the chief results of the classical literary criticism as represented by the JEDP (classification) scheme (see above, p. 3, n. 3), Alt emphasizes, in the introduction to 'Origins . . .' (pp. 81-88), that the methods evolved by literary criticism are unsuitable for an exact analysis of the collections of laws in the Old Testament. A direct line can be traced from this standpoint to the thesis of Henning Graf Reventlow in his work, *Das Heiligkeitsgesetz*, 1961, p. 166, to the effect that the collections of laws in the Old Testament (Lev. 17-26 is a case in point) are not literary compositions but the result of cultic and liturgical activities. For this reason Reventlow believes that literary criticism cannot 'proceed on its way unencumbered by form criticism', and that form criticism for its part cannot without further ado build on the foundations laid by literary criticism.

[23] 'Origins . . .', p. 117, n. 95.

[24] Cf. above all *Le Décalogue*, 1927, pp. 141-162. While Mowinckel's thesis has not lacked opponents (cf. for example Joachim Begrichs' rejection of it in *Die*

is that it finally solves the problem of the context in which such decalogues would originally have been proclaimed. The psalm concerned begins with the question who can be permitted to enter the sanctuary as a guest. We encounter the same question in Ps. 24, of the character of which as a festal psalm (or better as a festal liturgy, an antiphony sung alternately by two groups) there can be no doubt. For according to Mowinckel the question concerning right of access to Mount Zion is put by those participating in the festal procession, who desire to enter the sacred area. And the answer is given by the priests guarding the door in the form of a priestly instruction. Thus it is a question of the conditions that are necessary for entering upon the sacred area. What is of special interest in Ps. 15 is that the priestly instruction in vv. 2-5 comprises ten commandments. Thus the decalogue of Ps. 15.2-5 appears to represent the entrance tora by means of which one seeking to enter the temple had to put his heart and reins to the test before he dared to set foot upon the sacred area. Now if this is correct it follows that the decalogue of the classic type may have had a somewhat similar function, although Mowinckel has to conclude that *the* decalogue itself was never composed for cultic use, and in all probability emerged in the late Assyrian period in the circle of Isaiah's disciples.

Finally we must also mention a parallel from the prophetic literature, namely Ezek. 18.5-9. This passage comes, of course, from a prophet who is rooted in the priestly tradition. Mowinckel drew attention to it as early as 1924,[25] asking whether it was a sheer coincidence that it consisted of a series of twelve commandments. Since then the passage, with its prophetic declaration of 'individual retribution', has often been regarded as a milestone in the history of the development of the Israelite-Jewish religion and has been recognized as throwing an im-

priesterliche Thora, 1936, p. 68, n. 1, and pp. 79f., n. 10) J. J. Stamm is still right in characterizing it (see his survey of researches in *TR*, NF 27, 1961, pp. 195ff.; cf. also *The Ten Commandments in Recent Research*, pp. 28ff.) as a decisive turning-point in research into the decalogue. Cf. also Klaus Koch 'Tempeleinlassliturgien und Dekaloge', in *Studien zur Theologie der alttestamentlichen Überlieferungen G. v. Rad zum 60 Geburtstag*, 1961, pp. 45-60.

[25] *Psalmenstudien V, Segen und Fluch in Israels Kult und Psalmdichtung*, 1924, pp. 107 and 117ff.

portant light on form-critical study of Israelite law.[26] The
catalogue of deeds from which a just man must refrain, and of
those which he must perform in order to maintain his righteousness, are repeated in vv. 10-13 and 14-17. The collection,
with its thirteen prohibitions and commands, all composed in
a terse formal style, has been of interest to form-critical research not only as providing a parallel to the decalogues and
dodecalogues mentioned above, but also because of the 'de-
claratory formula' in v. 9 with which the series concludes: He
who follows these maxims of righteousness (in the spheres of
cultic, moral and social and charitable behaviour) is declared
'righteous', *ṣaddīq*, and at the same time it is given to him to
hear an assurance of 'life': *ḥāyō yîhᵉye*, 'he shall surely live', cf.
v. 17. Of him whose behaviour is contrary to this—who trans-
gresses these commandments—the declaration is *mōt yūmāt*, 'he
shall surely die', v. 13, a formula which is familiar to us from
apodictic law.[27] The assurance of 'life' with which the priest-
prophet Ezekiel concludes the catalogue points in the direction
of a cultic or religious setting. It is a reflection of the assurance
which the priest gives in the name of Yahweh to the visitor to
the temple once that visitor has put himself to the test, measuring his conduct by the 'list of transgressions' (*Beichtspiegel*, lit.
'confessional mirror') with which he is confronted in the
catalogue.[28] Moreover this reply on the part of the priest is, in

---

[26] See the survey of relevant literature in Zimmerli, *Ezechiel*, 1958, p. 391. Also
Klaus Koch, 'Tempeleinlassliturgien und Dekaloge', pp. 56ff.

[27] Alt points to the series of *mōt yūmāt* commandments in Ex. 21. 12, 15-17 and
22.18 (+19) as typical statements of apodictic law. Cf. 'Origins . . .', pp. 111ff.

[28] The expression *Beichtspiegel*, used of declarations of innocence such as that in
Ezek. 18.5ff. and of examples of the entrance tora such as those in Ps. 15 and Ps.
24. 3ff. goes back to Kurt Galling, 'Der Beichtspiegel. Eine gattungsgeschichtliche
Studie', *ZAW* 47, 1929, pp. 125-130. He had a forerunner in Bernhard Duhm,
Die Psalmen, 1899, p. 41. Here the heading to the treatment of Ps. 15 runs: 'A sort
of confessional declaration (*Beichtspruch*) which may have been made in the course
of preparations for participating in the liturgy or sung during processions to the
holy mountain or at the commencement of the liturgy.' Duhm's late dating of the
psalms is in this connection irrelevant. In his book *Offersang og Sangoffer*, 1951,
p. 334, Mowinckel adopted the expression, translating it 'Skriftespeil' and applying it initially to Ps. 101 [ET omits]. In this he was influenced by the 'negative con-
fessions' which are to be found both in Akkadian royal rituals and in the Egyptian
Book of the Dead. As the counterpart of the declaration of innocence we may
compare the reproaches which the unsuccessful son of King Keret utters against

the last analysis, an assurance that the individual concerned *ipso facto* participates in the benefits ensuing from fellowship in the cult and union with God.[29] With the declaration of the penalty in v. 13 we find ourselves at the same time directly confronted with the problem of the relationship of apodictic law to the cult.[30]

Ezek. 18.5ff. would have a special interest for us if it could be shown with some degree of probability that underlying the existing twelve to thirteen commandments a 'decalogue' lay concealed. In v. 6 four concrete prohibitions are clearly expressed: (1) against sacrificial repasts on the mountains, (2) against image worship, (3) against adultery, (4) against intercourse with a menstruating woman. Verse 7 is introduced by a prohibition, (5) 'Thou shalt not oppress any man'. The next clause in the sentence runs 'thou shalt restore his pledge'. Since this clause refers back to the preceding one by the use of 'his' it cannot be an independent prohibition, but must rather be considered as a special instance of the kind of oppression which is prohibited. The sixth commandment is represented by the prohibition of robbery, and the seventh and eighth by the commandments to feed the hungry and clothe the naked. The ninth and tenth commandments are the prohibitions of lending at interest and usury in v. 8. But probably the remainder of v. 8 is to be understood as comprising two concrete commandments, the eleventh, to withdraw one's hand from iniquity and

his father in the Ugaritic texts (cf. II K VI 45ff.): 'Thou dost not take up the cause of the widow, thou dost not give justice to the oppressed, thou dost not pursue those that despoil the poor, thou dost not shelter the orphan at thy feet.' It should also be noticed that the threat of being condemned to the underworld is joined to these reproaches. For a fuller understanding of the question cf. Hammershaimb, 'On the Ethics of the Old Testament Prophets', *VTS* VII, 1960, p. 91.

[29] Identity of cultic fellowship, union with God and life is a general feature in the thought of the Old Testament psalms. Cf. G. von Rad, ' "Righteousness" and "Life" in the Cultic Speech of the Psalms', *The Problem of the Hexateuch and Other Essays*, ET, 1966, pp. 243-266. Von Rad has also recognized the profound theological significance which passages such as Ezek. 18 and its parallels in the Psalms possess as background material for Gen. 15.6 and also for the Pauline doctrine of justification. Cf. his article, 'Die Anrechnung des Glaubens zur Gerechtigkeit', *TLZ* 76, 1951, cols. 129-132.

[30] See below pp. 68ff. and pp. 130f.

the twelfth, to execute true justice between man and man. The repetitions of this 'dodecalogue' in vv. 10-13 and 14-17 contain variations which are supposedly deliberate. The first repetition contains only eight clauses while the second has thirteen. It is the first enumeration in vv. 6-8, therefore that must be adhered to. In this the positive formulation of the seventh and eighth clauses in the midst of a series of prohibitions might tempt one, from the form-critical point of view, to explain both these commandments (to give food to the hungry and clothing to the naked) as actually being a prophetic addition to an ancient series of ten.[31]

4. THE ORIGINALITY OF THE NUMBER TEN
IN EXODUS 20 AND DEUTERONOMY 5

In the preceding sections we have encountered numerous difficulties in connection with the number ten. We found it difficult to establish any really definite symbolic value attached to the number ten. We also found it difficult to point to any one of the traditional methods of enumerating the decalogue as the only correct one, at least on the basis of the existing formulation of the ten commandments in Ex. 20 and Deut. 5. We looked for analogies to the decalogue both inside and outside the Pentateuch, but concerning the actual number ten none of them was *immediately* enlightening. Hence there are very good grounds for raising the question whether it is really correct to follow the Deuteronomists (cf. Deut. 4 and 10) in applying the number ten to our 'ten commandments'.[1]

[31] Zimmerli (*Ezechiel*, p. 404) has thoughts tending in this direction. As I see it the overall plan of the series is quite clear once one allows that after the eight negative formulations 8b ('. . . withholds his hand from iniquity'), which is negative in character but positive in formulation, serves as a transition to the tenth commandment, '. . . executes true justice between man and man'. The *content* of the two purely positive clauses cannot be said to support the view that they represent a later post-prophetic precision. The passage from the Ugaritic texts cited on p. 25, n. 28, shows how well attested the idea was in ancient times, that the 'righteous' had a duty towards the hungry (and the naked).

[1] Deut. 4.13: 'And he declared to you his covenant which he commanded you to perform, that is the ten commandments; and he wrote them upon two tables of stone.' 10.1-5: 'At that time Yahweh said to me: Hew two tables of stone like the

The impression cannot be avoided that the Deuteronomists have been greatly concerned to ensure that the collection of laws which they present in Deut. 5.6-21 really shall be accepted as a decalogue, the words of which are divided between two tables. In 4.13 the passage in question is directly called the 'covenant' of Yahweh, 'the ten words' (RSV margin), and in ch. 5 it is immediately preceded by an introduction, vv. 1-5, which defines more precisely the significance of these words of the covenant for later generations. In Deut. 10.1-5 we clearly sense a desire to eliminate all misunderstandings with regard to this passage. In this chapter it is expressly stated that the words recorded here are identical with those written on the tables which Moses had to prepare afresh after he had smashed the first pair of tables in his anger at the apostasy of Aaron and the people in the episode of the dance round the 'golden calf'. These words are therefore the same as the words of those first tables also. It was precisely the ten words of the first covenant, 5.6ff., which were recorded on the tables, and it was after this recording that these tables acquired their permanent place in the 'ark of the covenant' (10.2, 5). It is not inconceivable that the misunderstanding against which we are being warned may consist in regarding some collection of laws other than the

---

first and come up to 'me on the mountain and make an ark of wood ('*arōn*, literally 'box') and I will write on the tables the words that were on the first tables, which you broke, and you shall put them in the ark. So I made an ark of acacia wood and hewed two tables of stone like the first and went up the mountain with the two tables in my hand. And he wrote on the tables, as at the first writing, the ten commandments which Yahweh had spoken to you on the mountain out of the midst of the fire on the day of the assembly, and Yahweh gave them to me. Then I turned and came down from the mountain and put the tables in the ark which I had made, and there they are, as Yahweh commanded me.' In their version of the story of how the ark was brought into the Holy of Holies at the consecration of Solomon's temple (see above, p. 8, n. 6) the Deuteronomists are no less eager to emphasize that the tables were contained in the ark: 'There was nothing in the ark except the two tables of stone which Moses put there at Horeb, where Yahweh made a covenant with the people of Israel when they came out of the land of Egypt', I Kings 8.9. As Gressmann rightly observes, in reading this passage the suspicion arises that the Deuteronomists are here consciously contesting a view which maintained that the ark *did* contain something else. Gressmann's own suppositions (most recently stated in *Die älteste Geschichtsschreibung und Prophetie Israels*, 2nd ed., 1921, p. 213), to the effect that originally the ark contained a male and a female divine image, belongs to the realm of wishful thinking in the 'history of religions' school.

'classic decalogue' itself as 'the words of the covenant' and possibly as 'the ten commandments'. Certainly this very mis-understanding could easily arise in connection with Ex. 34.14-28. In point of fact the misunderstanding against which we are being warned is that interpretation which was subsequently put forward in the theories of Goethe and Wellhausen. Now, as I see it, it is difficult to decide whether the tradition contained in Ex. 34.14-28 had already been fixed in writing precisely in its present form when the words of Deut. 4 and 10 were first formulated. While it is true that even Deuteronomy presupposes more than one of the traditions which we encounter in the first four books of the Pentateuch—many of them, moreover, in their existing formulation—yet from a literary point of view we should envisage two distinct works, the 'Tetrateuch' (Gen.-Num.) and the Deuteronomist history. Deuteronomy itself re-presents the introduction to this latter work, and is accordingly followed by the Books of Joshua, Judges, I and II Samuel and I and II Kings.[2] Now if Ex. 34.14-28 was already in existence in written form before the work of the Deuteronomists, it is perhaps possible to explain the energy with which the Deuter-onomists emphasize that the ten words are the 'classic' and not the 'cultic' decalogue. This would have arisen from their awareness that according to the older and sounder tradition the ten words of the covenant were none other than the 'classic' decalogue, which had wrongly been forced to give place to the 'cultic' one. To turn to the concrete historical facts: the Deuter-onomists complete their history about 560 BC, i.e. at a period when the sanctuary of Jerusalem has been destroyed. To the most recent sections of this history belong, presumably, those sections in Deuteronomy itself which are addressed to the people in the second person plural—to be exact, 4.11-14, 5.1-5 and 10.1-5.[3] At a time when the temple was already destroyed a certain interest may have arisen in the question of

---

[2] This traditio-historical view, in which the author of the present work shares, was first developed by Noth, *Überlieferungsgeschichtliche Studien I*, 1943, and inde-pendently of him by Ivan Engnell, *Gamla Testamentet* (The Old Testament) 1945, the latter author maintaining a hostile attitude towards literary criticism.

[3] On this question see below, pp. 46ff.

what was, and what was not the true basis of Yahweh's covenant with Israel. On the one hand it would have been natural at such a time to *affirm* that the basis of it was that 'decalogue' which contained not a single word concerning the temple cult or the yearly pilgrimage festivals, that is, the decalogue of Ex. 20 (=Deut. 5). On the other hand it would have been natural to *contest* the idea that the covenant of Yahweh with Israel was based upon a collection of covenant words that gave particular prominence to the temple cult and pilgrimage festivals. Historically speaking the special interest of the Deuteronomists would have been justified *if* it was in fact the case that the 'cultic decalogue' had usurped the place which *properly* belonged to the 'classic decalogue' at a time when the Jerusalem temple was still standing.

In that case, however, where does the cultic decalogue belong? On this point the answers usually offered by the literary critics fail to satisfy. It is here suggested that up till now they have been so over-preoccupied in their researches with the combination 'J' (the Yahwist, often assigned to the period before the great prophets) and the 'cultic decalogue' of Ex. 34.14ff. that they have altogether missed the distinctive characteristics of the cultic decalogue itself. Let us take the great emphasis which it lays upon the duty of making pilgrimage. Three times a year every male person in Israel must appear before 'the Lord, Yahweh, the God of Israel', i.e. at the central sanctuary. No historical context fits this prescription so well as does that of the reform of Josiah, and the circumstances of this reform afford the most natural explanation of it. In 622 BC at the instigation of the king an attempt was made to subordinate all *legitimate* forms of the cult of Yahweh to the royal sanctuary at Jerusalem and to extirpate all *illegitimate* forms. Now at least four of the stipulations contained in the cultic decalogue are directly related to the particular annual festival which became the predominant one as a result of this reform, namely Passover.

Some have taken the words 'the ten commandments' in Ex. 34.28b as a secondary addition to the words immediately preceding, 'And he wrote upon the tables the words of the covenant'.[4] However a factor which speaks decisively against this view is the difficulties which, as we have seen, are involved in fitting the complex of Ex. 34.14ff. into a 'ten-word' structure.[5] It is here suggested that for this juxtaposition of 'covenant words' and 'ten commandments' which we meet in Ex. 34.28b only *one* meaningful explanation can be found: this juxtaposition was already firmly rooted in tradition before the context in which we now find it in Ex. 34 was composed in connection with Josiah's reform.[6]

From what has been said above, based though it admittedly is upon the theory that the Deuteronomists knew Ex. 34 in the form in which we have the text today,[7] it must be concluded that the energy with which the Deuteronomists seek to inculcate their message is to be explained as an attempt to revive a tradition earlier than Josiah and to make it fully recognized and respected.[8] If this is in fact the case, then we are justified

[4] Cf. Hans Kosmala, 'The So-Called Ritual Decalogue', *ASTI* I, 1962, p. 34: 'Somebody' appended the words 'the ten commandments', intending them as a commentary, but we do not know who was responsible for this 'unapt comment'. Kosmala has here correctly seen that the expression 'the ten words' refers to the classic decalogue, but it is inadmissible to strike out the words here as a gloss, the purpose of which cannot be explained.

[5] A glossator would have satisfied himself beforehand that the words in question were in fact immediately preceded by a decalogue. Cf. W. Rudolph, *Der 'Elohist' von Exodus bis Josua*, 1938, p. 59, n. 1.

[6] On the connection of the 'cultic decalogue' with the history of the golden calf and Josiah's reform see also below, p. 32, n. 12.

[7] This is altogether probable in view of the fact that the Deuteronomists, that is, those responsible for the final composition of the Deuteronomist history, are seen to be simply the party which took over the heritage of those responsible for Josiah's reform.

[8] Many theories have been put forward about the origin of the Deuteronomist movement (Bentzen: the 'country Levites'; von Rad: the *'am hā-'āreṣ* of Judah and their connection with the Levites; Alt: Northern Israelite circles). In my book, *Shechem*, 1955, pp. 345ff., I have, independently of von Rad and Alt, argued that the Deuteronomist movement arose from the taking over and further development of certain ancient 'democratic' traditions of the northern kingdom on the part of Jewish and Jerusalemite circles—a combination of opposites. It should be noticed that the earliest quotation from the decalogue for which a date can be assigned is to be found in Hosea (cf. Hos. 4.2), who lived in the northern kingdom in the period immediately before the fall of Samaria in 722 BC. This gives us good grounds for assuming that the earlier tradition of the decalogue (i.e. the classic decalogue) derives from Northern Israelite circles. The connection between the decalogue and the ark of the covenant is rightly regarded as a typical Deuteronomist *theologumenon*. It is suggested that what is presupposed here is not only the taking over of

in taking into account the fact that the connection between the number ten and the 'classic decalogue' is significantly older than the passages in which it is explicitly attested, namely Deut. 4 and 10, which belong to the period of about 560 BC. However, whether or not the Deuteronomists knew Ex. 34 in its present form, the energy with which they assert that it was none other than the 'classic decalogue' which was identical with the ten words of the covenant kept in the ark can be explained in another way. The complex of ideas which may be grouped under the heading 'Ark and Ten Words' may possibly have had a different genesis. We have noticed above that the number ten apparently played an important part in the sacred architecture of Jerusalem.[9] In another connection[10] we have offered certain reflections on the history of the ark of the covenant, and have expressed the view that the 'Priestly' description of the ark as 'ark of the testimony', *'arōn hā-'ēdūt*, is perhaps supported by a better tradition than the Deuteronomists' *'arōn habbᵉrīt*, the 'ark of the covenant'. In this connection we have adduced several elements of tradition which indicate that the ark had an important function in the royal temple of Jerusalem, not least in connection with the coronation of the king.[11] In all its long history the Deuteronomist movement never showed any extraordinary enthusiasm for the monarchy, least of all in its final stages when the monarchy had already come to an end. Now let us suppose that during the period of the monarchy, as part of the coronation rituals which took place in the temple, a coronation oracle of ten 'words' would have been pronounced, and that, as one must assume, the ark of the covenant would have played an essential part in this procedure. On this hypothesis it would be entirely comprehensible for the Deuteronomists to show a special interest in insisting that the 'ten words'

Northern Israelite traditions by Jewish and Jerusalemite circles, but the fall of Jerusalem and of the monarchy as well.

[9] See above pp. 7f.

[10] 'Some Reflections on the History of the Ark', *VTS* VII, 1960, pp. 61-74; cf. especially pp. 73f.

[11] The background for this hypothesis is to be found in the theory of the ark as the empty throne of God, which was first introduced to Old Testament research by M. Dibelius in his treatise *Die Lade Jahves*, 1906.

contained in the 'ark of the covenant' really were the classic
decalogue and not such a coronation oracle. Moreover, assuming that the present text of Ex. 34 may be regarded as an
expression of the aspirations which grew up among the insti-
gators of Josiah's reform,[12] these aspirations are to be regarded
only as the forerunners of the purely Deuteronomist ones. This
argument holds good quite independently of the question of
whether the Deuteronomists were in some degree correct in
maintaining that the number ten was firmly attached to the
cultic decalogue right from the outset, and so at a period earlier
than that of Ex. 34. The outcome of these considerations is that
the number ten, as it appears in the classic decalogue, has no
necessary connection whatever with symbolism such as might
be found to underly the architecture of the Jerusalem temple.
As it occurs in the decalogue the number ten is simply to
be explained as being, from a pedagogic point of view, the
supremely practical number, the number which a man could
count on his fingers.

The analogies to the decalogue point in the same direction.
It is true that hardly a single one of the passages included in this
examination[13] appears to be a decalogue. Yet of all the attempts
which we made to find decalogues either by form-critical or

[12] In the work referred to above W. Rudolph shows himself a supporter of the
view that the 'cultic decalogue', which he rightly refuses to recognize as a decalogue,
is secondary in its present position, having taken over the place once occupied by
the 'classic decalogue'. He explains this changing of the place of the classic decalogue as an attempt to give it a stronger and more prominent position. For the
insertion of the narrative of the golden calf had had the effect of making the classic
decalogue seem too remote from its previous context in the work as a whole. In
the lacuna thus left by its removal the 'ritual decalogue' was inserted as a 'stopgap'
(*op. cit.*, pp. 58-61). This explanation strikes one as based far too much upon theory.
For what are the practices against which the story of the golden calf is polemically
directed? Whatever else those practices may be they must include the cult of Bethel,
which was so strongly condemned in certain circles. Again what were the chief
aims of Josiah's reform? To centralize the cult at Jerusalem, to abolish all rival
sanctuaries, and most especially the most dangerous rival of all, namely Bethel,
and to some extent to make amends to the Levitical priesthood. In II Kings 23.15
the destruction of the temple at Bethel by King Josiah is explicitly described. The
narrative of the golden calf culminates in the consecration of the Levitical priesthood; to this is appended the account of Moses' proceedings on the occasion when
the covenant was renewed—and this is followed in 34.14ff. by the 'cultic decalogue'.

[13] Ps. 15 represents, perhaps, an exception to this. Since the research into the
psalms by Gunkel and Mowinckel, and since the appearance of Mowinckel's *Le*

traditio-historical methods in Deut. 27, Lev. 18 and 20 or Ezek. 18, none of them were merely arbitrary. A certain support was found ready to hand in the actual texts concerned. We therefore share in the opinion that these analogies provide the strongest support for regarding Ex. 20 and Deut. 5 as a collection of laws consisting of exactly ten commandments.

The fact still remains, however, that both these passages, even if the mutual variations between them are disregarded, cannot be fitted into an ordered scheme of exactly ten commandments altogether without strain. However once we undertake to recover the presumed original form of the decalogue this difficulty disappears. We shall be returning to this question later (in chapter III).

5. THE POSSIBLE DISTRIBUTION BETWEEN THE TWO TABLES

We have already mentioned the difficulties involved in enumerating the ten commandments of the classic decalogue as it now exists in a manner which is both irrefutable and enlightening. But the distribution of the 'ten commandments' in their present form between the two tables undoubtedly involves difficulties too.

At first sight a division of the commandments into two groups of five might seem the most suitable. But on this hypothesis, if we take as our basis the present form of the decalogue the first table would have to contain 139 verbal units[1] while 24 would have to suffice for the second. A different distribution has been suggested by Augustine. He would assign the first three commandments to the first table and the seven remaining ones to the second. This is the distribution which has become traditional in the Catholic and Lutheran Churches. From a mathematical

---

Décalogue, 1927, this psalm has played an essential part in research into the decalogue.

[1] By verbal units I mean groups of letters separated graphically either by an interval or by a hyphen or *meteg*. The figure of 139 units is arrived at on the basis of Ex. 20 according to Augustine's enumeration. As enumerated by Calvin the corresponding numbers are 137 and 26.

point of view this distribution is more satisfactory: 122 units on the first table, 41 on the second. Manifestly however symmetry is not achieved even here. For Augustine considerations of this kind are not decisive. His division is based rather upon content: the first to the third commandments (according to his own enumeration) are concerned with man's relationship with God, and the fourth to the tenth commandments with his relationship with his neighbour.

In the course of time numerous other attempts have been made to distribute the commandments between the two tables,[2] but it is unnecessary to investigate these more closely at this point. A factor which is common to them all, which carries conviction of itself, and which is, moreover, from a form-critical point of view entirely reasonable is that they all attempt to rid the existing text of 'later additions' and to reduce the individual commandments to short formulae.

The line of thought which we have developed in this section leads us to conclude that there is no reason to lay special emphasis on a supposed division of the decalogue into two parts. Assuming that the references to two tables of stone in connection with the decalogue are in fact supported by sound tradition, it is suggested that this is adequately accounted for by recalling that a man's ten fingers are divided between his two hands. But it is extremely probable that the two tables were from the outset connected with the temple, ark of the covenant and coronation ceremony, and that it was only subsequently that they were transferred to the context of the ritual decalogue and later still to that of the classic one.[3]

[2] We have mentioned above the attempts of Ernst Meier (see above p. 13, n. 6 and below pp. 78f.) and of Hans Schmidt (see above p. 12, n. 3 and further on this pp. 79f.).

[3] If one might venture a conjecture as to what was probably inscribed on the two tables of the ark of the testimony, it would be tempting to point to the most unmistakable example of a coronation psalm in the entire collection of the Old Testament psalms, namely Ps. 110. This is clearly divided into two and presented in the form of two oracles (vv. 1-3, 4-7). Jachin and Boaz (I Kings 7.15-22), the two freestanding stone pillars set before the temple at Jerusalem have certainly a ritual significance. It is possible that their names represent the opening words of oracles promising long life and power to the dynasty.

II

THE LITERARY PROBLEM OF THE
DECALOGUE

I. TEXTUAL AND LITERARY COMPARISON OF
EXODUS 20 AND DEUTERONOMY 5

20.1: The decalogue is preceded by a short introductory sentence (v. 1a) setting it in its context: 'And God spoke all these words saying.' In place of this the decalogue of Deut. 5 has as its introduction the section of text mentioned above (characterized) by the use of the plural, v. 4, which emphasizes the point that the covenant has been made not only '. . . with our fathers, but with us who are all of us here alive this day' (v. 3). Nevertheless it is most probable that the Deuteronomists were familiar with the opening of Ex. 20.1a for they conclude the decalogue with a sentence that is all but identical with it: 'These words Yahweh spoke to all your assembly at the mountain . . .,' Deut. 5.22. We may note that the LXX, Targumim and Vulgate read 'Yahweh' instead of 'God' in Ex. 20.1a, presumably in an attempt to harmonize it with Ex. 19.24.

20.2: The text of Exodus is identical with that of Deuteronomy. The expression 'house of bondage' (Luther: '*Diensthaus*', 'house of servitude') is characteristic both for the original Deuteronomy and for the Deuteronomists.

20.3: In MT and Peshitta the text of Ex. 20 is identical with that of Deut. 5. LXX B translates '*al-pānāy* in Deuteronomy literally by πρὸ προσώπου μου, cf. Vulgate: *in conspectu meo*. The corresponding phrase in Exodus, on the other hand, is rendered by πλήν, 'beside', cf. Peshitta *lebar men(i)*. LXX A and F have this rendering also in Deuteronomy. The expression 'other gods' is frequent in the work of the Deuteronomists.

20.4: Here it is noteworthy that a *waw* has been inserted in the text of Ex. 20, while in Deuteronomy the words 'or any likeness' are attached as an asyndeton to the prohibition of images. Presumably it is the latter text that is the better, and the text in Ex. 20 is an example of stylistic polishing. The prohibition of images is thus presented in two forms, and it is *possible* to give a distinct interpretation to each: Deuteronomy: 'Thou shalt not make to thyself any divine image in the form of anything whatsoever', etc., and Exodus: 'Thou shalt not make to thyself any divine image or any likeness of anything', etc. Thus the Exodus version may be directed against the art of making images in all its forms.

20.5: Regardless of the masoretic vocalization *tā 'ābdem*, which is often taken to be a Hoph'al form, 'to make oneself a servant', the versions have taken the form as Qal. This is possible even if the masoretic vocalization is upheld, cf. forms in the Qumran texts such as *yᵉdōrᵉšūhū* (1 QS VI, 18 and 1QSa, II, 10). The Nash papyrus has the word for jealous in the less usual form *qannō'* (cf. Josh. 24.19; Nahum 1.2), while both Exodus and Deuteronomy give the form as *qannā'*. In Exodus the words *'al šillᵉšīm wᵉ'al ribbᵉ'īm* are attached as an asyndeton to *'al banīm* with the result that *banīm* here has the force of 'descendants'. On this point the Nash papyrus supports the Exodus reading against that of Deuteronomy, which prefixes a *waw* to *'al šillᵉšīm*. Thus in Deuteronomy the *banīm* are the children while *šillᵉšīm* refers to the grandchildren. This is contrary to the usage in Ex. 34.7, where *bᵉnē-banīm*, 'grandchildren', is interposed between *banīm* and *šillᵉšīm*. Here the text of Exodus is preferred. Syntactically the concluding phrase *lᵉśōn'āy* 'those that hate me' gives the impression of being a later appendage, especially in view of the fact that from the context it must refer to 'the fathers'. Together with Ex. 20.6 (Deut. 5.10) it must be regarded as a subsequent insertion in the text, written under the influence of Ex. 34.7 and parenetic in style. Here in Ex. 20.6 (Deut. 5.10) *lā'ᵃlāpīm* has almost been forced to bear the meaning of 'a thousandfold', while the translation 'unto thousands' in Ex. 34.7 is quite in place.

20.7: The only text-critical point to be noted here is that in
v. 7b LXX B has the name of God in its full form, κύριος ὁ
θεός σου, while A, F follow MT. With regard to the rendering
of Hebrew *lᵉšāw'* in the versions, the Peshitta comes closest to
the sense of the Hebrew word with its *bᵉdagaluta*, 'deceitfully',
while LXX with its ἐπὶ ματαίῳ, 'futilely', and the Vulgate with
its *frustra, in vanum* and *super re vana* prepare the way for the
modern interpretation, which takes the command as forbidding
the unconsidered or careless use of the name of God, e.g. in
expletives or in swearing and cursing. It should further be
noted that the transition from v. 6 to v. 7 is simultaneously the
transition from the speech of Yahweh in the first person singular
(Ex. 20.2-6) to the promulgation of Yahweh's commands to
Israel in the third person through an intermediary appointed
to make known the law. The question is whether v. 7 in its basic
form was presented as Yahweh's direct speech. If this was in
fact the case for v. 7 it would also apply to all the commandments following it, not counting their secondary additions. If
it is concluded on form-critical grounds that the motivating
clause in 20.7b is an addition, and that the word *'ᵉlōhekā*, 'thy
God' after Yahweh in v. 7a represents a liturgical expansion of
the original text, then it is possible to regard the name Yahweh
in v. 7a as the error of a copyist who has misunderstood the
purpose of an original *yod* after *šēm*. This *yod* would originally
have been the pronominal suffix of the first person singular,
'et-šᵉmī, 'my name'. But the copyist would have taken it as an
abbreviation of the name Yahweh. We shall be returning to this
problem in our consideration of the original form of the
decalogue.

20.8: In the case of the sabbath commandment the diver-
gencies between Exodus and Deuteronomy become more
striking. *ka'ᵃšer ṣiwwᵉkā Yahweh 'ᵉlōhekā* in Deuteronomy is
clearly a secondary expansion of the text. We encounter the
same formula in 5.16, again without support from Exodus. It is
also missing from the Nash Papyrus. Yet the expansion must
have been made at an early date and it is entirely consonant
with the general presentation of the Deuteronomic law as a

repetition, expansion and further precision of the Sinai law, making it applicable to the heart. It seems more difficult to decide between *zākōr*, 'recall' in Ex. 20 and *šāmōr*, 'observe' in Deut. 5, as to which is the original reading. Here the claims of *zakōr* are upheld as being the more unusual expression. An impression of the manner in which the Deuteronomists use this verb is gained from 5.15: it is important to bear in mind the favours which Yahweh has bestowed in history. Besides this, a fleeting glance at the concordance reveals that *šāmar* is the preferred word in Deuteronomy and the Deuteronomist history for observing the law. It is therefore easy to see how a *zākōr* would have come to be interchanged with a *šāmōr*. The nearest syntactical parallel to Ex. 20.8 occurs in Ps. 103.18, where the expression *l^ezokrē pīqqudāw la'^asōtām*, 'those who remember his commandments so that they do them' is parallel to *l^ešom^erē b^eritō*, 'those who observe his covenant'. The nearest parallel in content is to be found in the introduction to the Passover law, Ex. 13.3: *zakór 'et-hayyōm hazzē*, 'remember this day', a phrase which, moreover, follows upon a section of 'salvation history' written in the Deuteronomist style.

20.9: A continuation of the positive exhortation of v. 8: work must be carried out on the six work days. The development of the idea of the sabbath rest in the following verses presupposes this. No problems of textual criticism.

20.10: The natural way of taking MT here and in the parallel passage of Deuteronomy is to regard *yōm hašš^ebi'ī*, 'the seventh day' as the subject of a defining clause with *šabbat* as its predicate. This way of taking it brings out the word-play most fully. LXX and Vulgate have taken *yōm hašš^ebi'i* as an adverbial accusative, and translated 'on the seventh day'. Cf. on this the Nash Papyrus: *ubayyōm hašš^ebī'ī*, 'and on the seventh day'. The Peshitta follows MT. With regard to the remainder of the verse Exodus offers a shorter and, in our opinion, a more original form than Deuteronomy, while the Nash Papyrus betrays the influence of the longer form in Deuteronomy. And while the Peshitta follows MT faithfully (cf. also the Vulgate), LXX in its rendering of the text of Exodus carries over an element of the

Deuteronomy form in the words ὁ βοῦς σου καὶ τὸ ὑποζύγιόν σου
and by setting the word πᾶν before κτῆνος. 'Thine ox and thine
ass' is a typical secondary expansion of the passage. However
the addition which occurs at the end of the verse in Deuteronomy merits greater interest: 'that your manservant and your
maidservant may rest as well as you.' From the immediately
preceding list of those who are to enjoy the sabbath rest two
representatives are taken here to act almost in the manner of
points on a railway, guiding the development of ideas onto the
the 'track' of salvation history. Thus in Deut. 5.15, following
on immediately from this secondary addition, we find: 'You
shall remember that you were a servant in the land of Egypt,
and Yahweh your God brought you out thence with a mighty
hand and an outstretched arm. Therefore Yahweh your God
commanded you to keep the sabbath day.'

20.11: In contrast to what precedes we find here a quite
different reason given: 'For in six days God made heaven and
earth, and the sea and all that is in them. And he rested the
seventh day; therefore Yahweh blessed the seventh day and
hallowed it.' The literary critics generally maintain that the
motivation of the sabbath law in Ex. 20.11 presupposes the
'Priestly' (P) account of the creation in Gen. 1-2.4, and since
D (the Deuteronomists) is considered an older source than P,
the Deuteronomist form of the sabbath commandment is often
preferred as the older of the two. However this argument is
quite mistaken, and the problem confronting us here is particularly suitable to illustrate the inadequacy, and sometimes
too the impracticability of literary criticism in its classic form
when it is required to solve the literary and traditio-historical
problems of the Old Testament. We have seen that the sabbath
commandment (Ex. 20.8-10 and Deut. 5.12-14) is constructed
from three elements: first the basic commandment to keep the
sabbath holy, then a clause concerning work on the six other
days, and thirdly an insistence upon the fact that the sabbath
is a holiday on which all must rest. The reason given in Ex.
20.11 follows this sequence of ideas. Yahweh performed his
work in six days; on the seventh day he rested, and he declared

TC D

it holy. The reason given in Deuteronomy is far weaker because of the way in which it is formulated. The point of connection between the commandment and the reason for it here is simply the single pair, 'manservant and maidservant', taken from the list of those for whom work on the sabbath is prohibited. The reason which the Deuteronomists have decided to give for keeping the sabbath holy is therefore concerned not with the creation but with history. We have already seen that the elements constituting the framework of the decalogue in Deuteronomy represent one of the most recent strata in the Deuteronomist history writing. It follows that the background which we must take into account for the Deuteronomist version of the decalogue is presumably that period during which the people, even in impoverished Judaea, were languishing under the yoke of the Babylonian tyranny. Here we have clear grounds for altering the reason given for the sabbath commandment, and for finding it no longer in the history of creation, but in salvation history (*Heilsgeschichte*). The thought here is that in this period of darkness when Yahweh's ways are hidden, there is no other way into the future than to obey the law, to fear and to love Yahweh, and to be mindful of his favours in past history. Perhaps if this course is pursued he will once more accomplish a mighty deed and set his people free. We know from the prophecy of Deutero-Isaiah that upheavals in history could inspire a prophet to come forward and proclaim that *now* the time of the new exodus from the house of bondage had come. It is on the whole probable that the death of Nebuchadnezzar, the last major political event referred to (indirectly) in the Deuteronomist history writing (II Kings 25.27-30), inspired the Deuteronomists to bring their work, now one of the masterpieces of Old Testament literature, to its conclusion.

A further point is that the contention of the literary critics to the effect that Ex. 20.11 presupposes the Priestly Creation narrative, Gen. 1.1-2.4a, cannot be upheld. The Deuteronomist reason for the sabbath commandment concludes with a sentence which is not particularly adequate, and which is quite colourless: 'Therefore Yahweh your God commanded you to keep the sabbath day.' This sentence, with its explicatory '*al-kēn*, is clearly modelled upon Ex. 20.11, the final word of which represents an exemplary rounding off of the sabbath command as a whole. This final word is *wayyᵉqadᵉšēhū*, 'and he declared it holy'. It refers back to the formula by which the sabbath command is introduced in v. 8. Ex. 20.11 must therefore be pre-Deuteronomist, and it must be independent of the account of the creation in its existing formulation in Gen. 1.1ff., if the dating of the Priestly source in the post-Deuteronomist period is to be maintained. It is impossible at this point to discuss this entire question in all its complexity. But we can to some extent indicate that there are important differences between Gen. 1.1ff. (the use of *bārā'* for 'create', the fact that the sea is not created but = the primordial ocean that was there before the creation, the word *šābat* used of 'rest' from work) and Ex. 20.11. The striking similarity between Ex. 20.11 and Gen. 2.3 can therefore only be explained as due to the influence of the decalogue on the Creation narrative. By comparison Ex. 31.17 is far more closely connected with Gen. 1.1-2.4a. The historical question of whether the sabbath was originally a day of the week or of the month, and the question of what part it played in the history of Israel's and Judah's formation and cult is obviously of decisive importance if the date of the decalogue is to be determined. We shall be returning to these questions later in another connection.[1]

20.12: In addition to the expansion spoken of above in Deut. 5.16 Deuteronomy contains a second expansion. The phrase *ūlᵉma'an yīṭab lāk*, 'and that it may go well with you' is added on to the words 'that your days may be prolonged'. The Nash Papyrus has the same addition, but placed *before* the words 'that your days may be prolonged', and we have the same text in LXX B for Ex. 20.12 and in LXX for Deut. 5.16. The change of position of the phrase 'that it may go well with you' is an indication, more or less certain from a text-critical point of view, that these words are an addition subsequently inserted in the text as a commentary on the words concerning length of

---

[1] Cf. pp. 101ff.

days. The days were to be not merely long but—still more important—happy too. The phraseology is plainly Deuteronomist, cf. Deut. 4.40; 5.26; 6.3, 18; 12.25, 28 and 22.7. The same is to some extent true of the phrases 'that your days may be prolonged' and 'in the land which Yahweh your God gives you'.

20.13f.: We have already touched upon the questions of textual criticism at an earlier stage. The sequence of briefly formulated commandments in MT is the same in Exodus and Deuteronomy, and in both passages the readings are upheld by the Peshitta and Vulgate. LXX A and F also have this sequence, but against this the prohibition of adultery is placed before that of killing in the Nash Papyrus as well as in Philo's *De Decalogo*, and also for Deuteronomy in LXX B. LXX B presents the commandments in the Exodus version in the following sequence: Adultery, theft, killing. That the prohibition of killing should come before that of adultery appears to us as obvious as it is difficult to explain why some witnesses to the text should give these two commandments in the opposite order. On grounds of intrinsic content we prefer the order attested by the Nash Papyrus, LXX B for Deuteronomy, and Philo.

20.16: Here the versions are unanimous in upholding the Exodus form, which speaks of '*ēd šāqer*, 'false testimony' or possibly 'lying witness', while Deuteronomy has '*ēd šāw*', a reading which is also found in the Nash Papyrus. On the word *šāw* see above under 20.7. This must be a case of 'remote assimilation' between Deuteronomy 5.20 and 5.11. This commandment is a prohibition of accusing others falsely when one appears as witness for the prosecution, and with regard to content it must be said that *šeqer* is in this context the most correct term.

20.17: Even though the Nash Papyrus has a small gap in the text at this point, it is certain that its reading followed that of the Deuteronomists and set the prohibition of coveting one's neighbour's wife before that of coveting his house. If the prohibition of covetousness is indeed to be divided into two commandments it is also preferable from the human and psychological standpoint to take the prohibition of coveting one's neighbour's wife as the primary and more important one. In this respect Augustine is human and psychological in outlook, while Luther remains set in an antiquated patriarchalism: 'Nemen sy den leyb, gut, ehr, kind und weyb . . .'[2] There can be no doubt that the Exodus form is the original one. The Deuteronomists have introduced a further secondary variation by using the verb *tit'awwe* instead of *taḥmōd*. This represents not merely a stylistic variation but an actual watering down of the prohibition to 'covet', *ḥāmad*. As E. Meier and later Johannes Herrmann (see above, p. 13, n. 6) have pointed out, the final commandment of the decalogue is a prohibition of appropriating what belongs to another. The remaining differences between Ex. 20 and Deut. 5 with regard to this commandment are of less interest since it can be established on form-critical grounds that all that comes after *bēt-rē'ekā*, 'your neighbour's house' in Ex. 20.17 represents secondary filling.

The results of our comparison of the texts of Ex. 20 and Deut. 5 are undoubtedly in favour of the version of Ex. 20. At one single point, Ex. 20.4, we have felt compelled to deviate from the form of text found in Exodus and to prefer the version of Deuteronomy because of the interpolation of a *waw* ('and') between the actual prohibition of images and the explanation which follows in the next few sentences. Stylistically this has a smoothening effect; as regards content it seems to impart a degree of precision which is uncharacteristic. At no point have we concealed the fact that on form-critical grounds we have had to accept that the decalogue, even in its earliest form in Ex. 20, has come down to us in a form which has been greatly worked over. To the indications which we have already given, most of which tend in the direction of striking out one clause after another as a secondary accretion, we may add a further observation. The prohibitions of adultery, killing and theft are, from a form-critical point of view, formulated too briefly. In addition to this the prohibition of theft in its present form over-

---

[2] 'And though they take our life,
Goods, honour, children, wife . . .'

laps, to some extent, with the concluding prohibition of the decalogue, that of appropriating another's possessions.

2. OUR PRESENT DECALOGUE IN ITS LITERARY FRAMEWORK

Before we proceed with our form-critical observations we have a further problem of literary criticism to discuss: How is the decalogue related to the sections of narrative which surround it in Ex. 19-34 or in Deut. 4-11.

It is as true of our present Deuteronomy as it is of the four preceding books of the Pentateuch that it cannot be considered as a unified work. It was not composed according to a single predetermined plan, or within the limits of a single narrowly defined period or by a single author or group of authors. Yet for all this a certain continuity can be discerned underlying the processes from which this work emerged, and this makes it easier to analyse than the other four books of the Pentateuch. Since in addition both forms of the classic decalogue bear the stamp of the Deuteronomist style, a fact which scholars have long recognized,[1] we have every justification for taking the decalogue in Deuteronomy and its literary framework first in the present consideration.

At an earlier stage we have discussed one of the most noteworthy deviations of the Deuteronomist version of the decalogue, namely the reason given for the sabbath commandment, and have explained this from the historical situation of the Deuteronomists themselves.[2] If this explanation is correct then it is clearly possible to discern the most recent stratum of the Deuteronomist writing in the distinctive form which the decalogue has acquired in Deuteronomy. This in turn would lead one to expect that the Deuteronomists have found it possible to place the decalogue in a context which brings out their own

---

[1] Cf. the examples of Deuteronomist language in both versions of the decalogue in our detailed survey of the decalogue text. That even Ex. 20.1ff. bears a strongly Deuteronomist stamp is one of the main contentions of O. Meisner's treatise, *Der Dekalog*, Leipzig, 1893, a work which is unfortunately inaccessible to me. Cf. H. Holzinger, *Exodus*, 1900, p. 69.   [2] See above pp. 39f.

purpose. That this is in fact what they have done will be clearly apparent to anyone who has followed the traditio-historical line in the more recent research. Applying the results of this to the subject under consideration we should regard Deut. 1-3 not as the particular introduction to Deuteronomy itself, or as one of the introductions to this book (as has so often been done by the exponents of literary criticism), but we should rather view these chapters as an introduction to the Deuteronomist historical work which extends from Deut. 1 to II Kings 25, but which from a *literary* point of view has nothing to do with the 'tetrateuch' (Genesis to Numbers). The brief summary provided in this Deuteronomist history of the narrative of the wilderness wanderings from the exodus to the arrival at the plains of Moab is based, as has long been established, on the same stratum of earlier traditions which the Priestly editor of the Tetrateuch has incorporated in his work.

But the Deuteronomists have taken three episodes from the traditions of the wilderness wanderings, namely the account of the conclusion of the covenant at Horeb, the decalogue and the episode of the golden calf, and have transferred this material to chs. 4-11. The fact that certain somewhat shocking features found in Exodus have been mitigated[3] merely serves to underline the Deuteronomists' dependence on the earlier material in Exodus. We have already touched upon the fact that some of this material has been omitted (notably Ex. 34).[4]

Deut. 4-11 is therefore presented as a monumental introduction to the distinctive Deuteronomist version of the laws which we find in Deut. 12-26. The text is suffused with religious zeal for Yahweh's interests. The style is kerygmatic (salvation history) and parenetic (observance of the law). Israel is exhorted to be faithful to Yahweh and to keep his law.

In the form in which this material has come down to us the decalogue occupies an apparently central place. Indeed it might seem as though the decalogue were the nucleus round

[3] Thus Aaron's share in the guilt of the apostasy is not directly referred to. We are merely told in Deut. 9.20: 'And Yahweh was so angry with Aaron that he was ready to destroy him. And I prayed for Aaron also at the same time.'

[4] Cf. pp. 26ff.

which the quite different material had crystallized. It is as though the Deuteronomists intended to say that no matter what the specific Deuteronomistic lawgiving (12-26) represented as Moses' testament on the plains of Moab—delivered immediately before his own death and the entry of the tribes into Canaan—one point is quite certain: the basic covenant between Yahweh and Israel was concluded at Horeb, and concluded not merely with the fathers but 'with us who are all of us here alive this day'. What it means for Yahweh to be Israel's God is expressed in the introduction to the decalogue (5.6): 'I am Yahweh your God, who brought you out of the land of Egypt and out of the house of bondage.' What it means for Israel to be Yahweh's people is stated in the individual commandments of the decalogue: the individual 'man of Yahweh' is one who reverences Yahweh alone, adores no image apart from him, does not profane his name, but keeps the sabbath, honours his parents, refrains from killing, adultery, stealing, false witness and appropriating the possessions of another. *That* is the content of the covenant, written on the tables which were laid in the ark of the covenant.

After the Deuteronomist laws have been set forth there follow in ch. 27 directions for the ceremony by which the covenant between Yahweh and Israel is to be confirmed on the soil of Canaan after the conquest of the land. To this is appended a number of blessings and curses (ch. 28) and a series of exhortations (chs. 29-30) as well as some words of farewell to the people and Joshua (31.1-8). Finally 31.9-13 comprises, as the conclusion of this entire complex, a directive to the Levites and elders that every seven years in the 'year of release' they are to assemble the people at the feast of Tabernacles and to read the law to them so that they may learn it.[5]

The alternation between the second person singular and the second person plural in the form of address to Israel in these

[5] On the significance of this passage for an understanding of apodictic law cf. p. 60. What follows after 31.13 consists for the most part of an introduction to the poetical texts of Deut. 32 and 33, and also the account of Moses' death, which represents the redactional link between the Deuteronomist history and the conclusion of the tetrateuch. See Noth, *Überlieferungsgeschichte des Pentateuchs*, 1948, p. 16.

framework passages has provoked one source-critical study after another over the last seventy years.[6] The apparently quite purposeless alternation between 'thou' and 'you' must surely have an explanation. Surely it must be possible by means of it to distinguish between the earlier and later elements in Deuteronomy. An analysis of Deut. 4ff. recently carried out on the basis of this criterion[7] has established, so far as we can judge, that this view is valid. The carefully worked out 'thou' passages are to be taken for the most part as the original introduction to the laws in Deut. 12-26, while the 'you' passages exhibit a clear connection with the introduction to the history in chs. 1-3, and are therefore probably to be considered as the most recent stratum, i.e. as the Deuteronomist 'editor's' own contribution. For our problem, namely the relationship of the decalogue to its literary framework, the conclusion of the relevant analysis is particularly interesting. All the passages which speak of or refer to the ten commandments, the ark and the stone tables belong to the 'you' complex, the most recent material used by the Deuteronomists. The only unusual feature is that the second person singular has been retained for the decalogue itself in its 'Deuteronomized' form.

What deductions can be drawn from the foregoing? A first deduction which is enlightening must be that the Deuteronomists after the fall of Jerusalem made really immense efforts to

[6] C. Steuernagel, *Die Rahmen des Deuteronomiums*, 1894, and W. Staerk, *Das Deuteronomium, sein Inhalt und seine literarische Form*, 1894, were the first to use this alternation between singular and plural as a criterion. Both accepted the existence of three continuous written sources. In the year 1947 J. H. Hospers undertook a fresh examination of the entire problem (*De Numeruswisseling in het Boek Deuteronomium*), and came to the conclusion (pp. 92ff.) that in its earliest form Deuteronomy was composed in the singular, but that not all the passages in the singular belong to this earliest form. He further concludes that the next stages of development are represented by a series of passages in the plural, in which an exile is clearly presupposed. This was probably the exile of the northern Israelite population after 722 (the fall of Samaria) rather than the Judahite exile (after 587, the fall of Jerusalem). Later additions were made about the time of Josiah's reform in 622 (Hospers says 621), and the final appendices, as for example the passage in 4.29-30 composed in the singular, clearly presuppose the fall of Jerusalem.

[7] G. Minette de Tillesse, 'Sections "tu" et sections "vous" dans le Deuteronome', *VT* 12, 1962, pp. 29-88. Her analyses in terms of literary criticism are based upon the traditio-historical foundation laid down by Noth in his treatment of the Deuteronomist history writing in *Überlieferungsgeschichtliche Studien* I, 1943.

give the 'classic decalogue' a central place in their tradition. That was precisely the impression immediately received from reading Deut. 4-11, namely that the sections of text preceding and following Deut. 5 were wholly orientated towards the decalogue. But the idea that the decalogue must have been the passage about which *all* the rest of the material crystallized as it were, now appears as in part illusory. It is valid for the later 'you' sections, but not *ipso facto* for the earlier 'thou' sections. For the rest it can only give us satisfaction that we have felt compelled to draw the deduction mentioned above. In fact it represents a support from the side of literary criticism for the hypothesis which we have developed above[8] on traditio-historical grounds with regard to the relationship between the 'cultic' and the 'classic' decalogues.

The next deduction which we might feel ourselves tempted to draw is less certain. It is that the decalogue, which is un-deniably composed in the second person singular, must have had its place in the original Deuteronomy (however, inciden-tally, one may conceive of the relationship of that document to Josiah's reform).[9] Of itself the fact that the decalogue is com-posed in the second person singular is hardly sufficient founda-tion for such a hypothesis. For it could well be that 'the deca-logue *as a type* was bound up with the 'thou' form, and that con-sequently this form had nothing to do with the passages in Deuteronomy in which the singular form of address predomin-ates.[10] The question might of course be raised whether the Deuteronomists, who have manifestly exercised an influence on the distinctive form of the decalogue which we encounter in

[8] Cf. pp. 27ff.

[9] Minette de Tillesse draws this conclusion, *op. cit.*, pp. 75ff., but she clearly recognizes some of the difficulties involved in it, cf. *op. cit.* p. 35. The decisive factor for her is that the decalogue in its present form is strongly marked by the attitudes which we encounter in the 'original Deuteronomy' (Ur-Deuteronomium). As will become apparent when we return to this question below, we find her line of argument unconvincing.

[10] W. Rudolph in *Der 'Elohist' von Exodus bis Josua*, p. 143, n. 2, contests the view that the classic decalogue would have been a secondary addition to our *present* Deuteronomy, and strongly emphasizes the connection between the decalogue and ch. 5 of Deuteronomy as a whole. For the Deuteronomists the 'thou' form was so inherent in the decalogue that it never occurred to them to depart from it in spite of the plural form of address in the rest of the chapter.

Deuteronomy, would not have disregarded the singular 'thou' and changed it into the plural if it really was they who were responsible for the inclusion of the decalogue in Deuteronomy. It is a fact that in Lev. 19.3-4 and 11-12 we find eight of the decalogue commandments which have been changed to the plural form: 'you shall not steal, you shall not lie', etc. However in determining to what extent the decalogue must have had a place in the original Deuteronomy the decisive factor must be whether more or less clear allusions to the decalogue are to be found in the rest of the 'thou' passages in Deut. 4-11, when all the 'you' passages have been excerpted.[11]

Admittedly in chs. 6-11 we often come across words and phrases in the 'thou' passages which are strongly reminiscent of the first and second commandments of the decalogue. For instance in 6.10-15 Yahweh is referred to as he 'who brought you out of the land of Egypt, out of the house of bondage' (v. 12). The people are exhorted to 'reverence him' (v. 13) (cf. the prohibition of reverencing other gods and idols in the decalogue). Yahweh is described as a 'jealous' God (v. 15) (cf. the reason given for the prohibition of images in the decalogue, Deut. 5.9). Again, in 6.6 we find to 'these words', *hadd⁰bārîm hā'ēle*, which Moses lays before the people 'today', the same expression as is used in the introductory formula of the decalogue in Ex. 20. But with regard to the first of these examples it is in reality a question of influence from the Deuteronomist side having been brought to bear on the linguistic constructions of the decalogue.[12] With regard to the use of *d⁰bārîm* as a designation for the commandments of the law, this is the very designation used for the decalogue in what is probably the earliest source material *outside* of Deuteronomy, while in Deuteronomy itself it occurs with a far wider range of meaning, being applied to all Yahweh's laws, including the specifically Deuteronomist ones.[13] In reality a closer analysis will show that it is far more

[11] In her otherwise excellent article Minette de Tillesse has not shown that any such allusions exist. [12] See above, pp. 35f.
[13] On this cf. especially the discussion by O. Grether, *Name und Wort Gottes im Alten Testament*, pp. 120-126: 'Das Deuteronomium und der dabar-Begriff.'

remarkable that in such short summaries of religious commandments as those in 6.13 and 10.20 we should encounter a formula
which appears to be totally uninfluenced by the decalogue:
'You shall fear Yahweh your God; you shall serve him and
cleave to him and swear by him' (or 'by his name'). Moreover
when one remembers the prominence accorded to the prohibition of images in the decalogue, then it is striking that the
word *pesel*, '(divine) image', should never occur at all in the
exhortations and warnings against religious decline in the
'thou' passages.

While therefore chs. 6-11 offer no grounds for the supposition
that the decalogue had its place in the original Deuteronomy,
the case is otherwise with ch. 4. But on this point the analysis
of this chapter is particularly difficult. It contains exhortations
in plural and singular alike, and it appears palpably evident
that some of the former presuppose the destruction of Jerusalem
and the deportation of part of the people to Babylon (v. 27).
Besides this some of the 'thou' passages appear as reasons for
exhortations which occur in the 'you' passages (vv. 24 and 31),
so that for this chapter the 'singular/plural' criterion is best
applied in a manner diametrically opposed to that which is
adopted for the rest of Deuteronomy. Verses 41-44 are best
taken as a historical note to the retrospective survey of the
Deuteronomists in Deut. 1-3, which belongs to the latest
stratum. Verses 44-49 still remain. Noth[14] regards these as an
introduction to the original Deuteronomy, while Minette de
Tillesse[15] would retain only v. 45 as the original introduction
to Deuteronomy. Chapter 4, which is for the most part a single
great paraphrase on the prohibition of images in the decalogue,
provides on this showing no evidence that the decalogue had its
place in the original Deuteronomy. In reality our analysis of
ch. 4 proves that the conclusion which we arrived at in connection with chs. 6-11 is valid. The supposition that the decalogue was a constituent element of the original Deuteronomy
is without foundation. Only the most recent traditions of

[14] *Überlieferungsgeschichtliche Studien* I, 1943, pp. 16ff.
[15] *Op. cit.*, p. 48.

Deuteronomy show connections with the ten commandments.

Let us turn then to Ex. 19-34, a section of text in which we find a combination of extremely late material[16] and earlier material, part of it very early. From this point of view the problems entailed in undertaking a literary analysis of the material certainly do not appear to be diminished. Source criticism in its classic form has found here a rich field of investigation, and while the correctness of many of the individual results which it has arrived at may be called in question, still it has been more or less established that literary analyses in some form are necessary if we are ever to extract any meaning from the text.

Let us consider first the immediate context of the decalogue. The existing arrangement of the material in Ex. 20.18-21 can be taken as the terrified reaction of the people to the mighty manifestation of God, which surrounded the proclamation of the ten commandments with lightning and thunder. Such, it seems, must have been the text which the Deuteronomists had before them, for in the passages preceding and following the decalogue in Deuteronomy (5.5 and 5.22f.) they speak of the fear which possessed the people as they witnessed the revelation of God amid fire and thunder. In terms of its subject matter Ex. 20.18-21 follows on from 19.16-21, verses which likewise speak of thunder, lightning and smoke, in terms which are in part identical.[17] But upon closer examination of the text of 20.18-21 the impression one receives is not that the people had been permitted to hear any epoch-making or final and eternal revelation, such as they themselves would have found sufficient to calm their fears—quite the reverse. They desire Moses to be the mediator of the divine revelation. Him they are willing to hear. If, on the other hand, they are forced to hear the words of God himself they will die (v. 19). Moses therefore calms the people and then turns to the dark cloud in which God is con-

[16] The literary critics' P material (especially chs. 25-31, but also 19.1f. and 24.15b-18).

[17] Only one who is totally and blindly devoted to literary criticism in its classic form could attach any importance to the alternation of the divine names which can be observed, as between Ex. 19.16ff. and Ex. 20.18ff., and also within individual verses in Ex. 19.16ff. In any case there are enough 'Elohim' verses in Ex. 19.16ff. to establish an organic connection with Ex. 20.18ff.

cealed. Following upon this in vv. 22ff. we have Yahweh's
words to Moses: 'Thus you shall say to the people of Israel:
you have seen for yourselves that I have talked with you from
heaven. You shall not make gods of silver to be with me, nor
shall you make for yourselves gods of gold.' The section immediately following, which is in the singular, is the so-called
'law of the altar', vv. 24-26. The sequence is further interrupted
by the Book of the Covenant (chs. 21ff.), a collection of casuistic
laws which have been augmented by large sections of apodictic
law. In other words we have here law-giving along the same
lines as the prohibition just cited against making images of
gods. It is clear then that with 21.1ff. an independent literary
complex begins: 'Now these are the ordinances, *mišpāṭîm*,
which you shall set before them' (21.1: 'you' here refers not to
the people, but to the law-giver, Moses). But however clear this
is, it is proportionately difficult to determine where the Book
of the Covenant ends, and, following upon this, where the list
of apodictic commands which began with the prohibition of
images in 20.23 is resumed. The casuistic *form* is maintained,
with interruptions, up to 23.5. This verse, together with v. 4, is
found in the midst of a short collection of apodictically formulated laws concerning the duty of judges to maintain true
justice (23.1-3, 6-9), a 'model for the judge', as the passage has
been called. It is self-evident that a book of laws[18]—and that is,
in effect, what the Book of the Covenant is—could hardly have
a more appropriate conclusion than this 'model for the judge'.
Besides this we have in Hammurabi's famous stele of laws the
finest analogy that could be desired. It must be remembered
that the Code of Hammurabi represents just such a compilation
of predominantly casuistic laws opening with a prologue couched
in solemn style, and closing with an epilogue no less solemn

[18] On the difference between 'Codex' and 'Book of Laws' cf. especially A. Jirku,
Das weltliche Recht im Alten Testament, 1927, pp. 13f.: A 'Codex' is a well-ordered
whole, a statement of the law deliberately planned and carried through, whereas
a 'Book of Laws' is a more or less accidental compilation of legal statutes. Jirku
describes the Book of the Covenant itself (p. 16) as a typical 'Book of Laws', but it
may be questioned whether it was not originally a 'Codex', the character of which
as Codex gradually faded out as a result of the numerous expansions (and perhaps
also omissions) which it must have had to undergo.

defining Hammurabi's task as king: 'to create justice in the land, to annihilate the wicked and the villainous in order that the mighty may not oppress the weak' (Col. 1, lines 33-39). It also speaks of his duty to protect the people so that 'the strong does not persecute the weak, and so that justice can be done to the widow and the orphan' (Col. 24, lines 59-62).

Now let us consider the complex of laws which follows upon the 'model for the judge', i.e. Ex. 23.10ff. If this can be attached to the conclusion of the 'law of the altar' in 20.26, the point at which the Book of the Covenant has been inserted, it is surely not unreasonable to suppose that the divine utterance, which is in reality announced in 20.18ff. as *about to commence*, is to be found in Ex. 20.22-26 plus 23.10-19. As has long been remarked, the subject matter of these verses is a self-contained complex which, both in form and content, represents the nearest conceivable parallel to the 'cultic decalogue' of Ex. 34.14ff.[19] The fact that the commandment which introduces this section of laws is formulated in the plural can be explained as an attempt to assimilate it to the narrative framework. Here the actual epic context itself, in which Moses is addressing the people, makes the plural form necessary. It appears hardly possible to decide with any certainty whether the 'cultic decalogue' of 34.14ff. or the collection of laws in 20.22-26 + 23.10-19 is to be regarded as the earlier.[20] But whichever it may be this collection

---

[19] Mowinckel discusses the question of the conditions for the institution of the covenant according to the 'Elohist' in *Le Décalogue*, 1927, pp. 36-43. He adds 22. 28-29 to the complex mentioned above, and finds in the whole a collection of twenty-four commandments in all. These are regarded as 'E's' conditions for the institution of the covenant and as identical with the Book of the Covenant mentioned in 24.7 as constituting an essential element in the ceremony of institution.

[20] In *Le Décalogue* Mowinckel is naturally compelled on the basis of his source-critical presuppositions to regard Ex. 34 (='J') as older than Ex. 20.23ff. +22.28f. +23.10-19 (='E'). In his article, 'The so-called Ritual Decalogue', *ASTI* 1, pp. 31-61, H. Kosmala carries out a detailed comparison between Ex. 34.18-24, entitled 'Text B', and Ex. 23.14-17, entitled 'Text A'. He considers both passages to be versions of an ancient festal calendar and appears—though he does not express any definite opinion on the question of the priority between them—to hold that Text B represents a secondary, more expanded 'edition' than Text A (p. 44). See further A. Jepsen, *Untersuchungen zum Bundesbuch*, 1927, pp. 99f. (see below, pp. 63f.); A. Eberharter, 'Besitzen wir in Exodus 23 und 34 zwei Rezensionen eines zweiten Dekalogs und in welchem Verhältnis stehen sie zu einander?', *BZ* 20, 1932, pp. 157-162.

of laws into which the Book of the Covenant has been inserted contains one ancient element which bears a special stamp. This is the 'law of the altar'. It prescribes that the altar of the Israelites shall be constructed of earth or possibly undressed stones, but under no circumstances of dressed stone, and hence[21] that it is not to be equipped with steps either. This prescription breathes the spirit of primitive ideas of taboo, which were associated with the holy places from very early times. And the protest it contains against the use of dressed stones is immediately intelligible as a protest against the improved techniques of building which were introduced into Israel under Solomon and with the development of urban culture (cf. I Kings 5.31; 6.36; 7.9, 11, 12 and Amos 5.11). This law, with its deeply significant phrase 'in every place where I cause my name to be remembered', is not only pre-Deuteronomist and pre-Josian, but may also contain a protest at this point against the centralizing tendencies introduced with the construction of the temple under Solomon.[22] 23.17, which admittedly contains a prescription which can hardly be taken in any other sense than as inculcating the duty of making pilgrimage to the central shrine at the three annual festivals, is in reality an interpolation from the 'cultic decalogue'. Not only is this verse almost verbally identical with 34.23, but it also constitutes a doublet with another directive about the three festivals which occurs *within* the same brief collection of laws, namely in 23.14. There is, however, one highly significant difference between 23.17 and 23.14. The latter passage only speaks of 'keeping a feast' three times a year. It does not say a single word about the duty of going on pilgrimage to a central sanctuary. Now in view of this there can be no further doubt that the collection of short 'words' of the covenant, which originally belonged to the

[21] The reason given in the existing text, namely 'that your nakedness be not exposed on it', is clearly secondary. Would such exposure be any more effectively avoided if a ramp were used? But perhaps what is prohibited is any kind of 'ascending' to the altar?

[22] On the 'law of the altar' and its possible connection with the 'Shechemite' tradition, cf. my book, *Shechem. A Traditio-Historical Investigation*, 1955, pp. 56-60, *et al.*

'Sinai/Horeb' pericope of Ex. 19-34, is to be found in Ex. 20. 22-26 + 23.10-19. It is imparted afresh in connection with the narrative of the apostasy at the foot of Sinai, i.e. the story of the 'golden calf', but in a form which is in harmony with Josiah's programme of reform. And the pilgrimage command with which we are concerned represents a weak echo of this in 23.17.

A second conclusion of our analysis is one which the reader will long since have anticipated. The existing 'classic' decalogue of Ex. 20.1-17 had originally no textual connection with Ex. 19-34.[23] That Book of the Covenant which plays an essential part in the ceremony of the making of the covenant as described in Ex. 24 must be our brief collection of laws consisting of the concluding verses of Ex. 20. and of Ex. 23.10ff. This must have been the case whether or not the 'book of laws' Ex. 21.1-23.9, which has in fact been joined to it, was originally included.

In answer to the question of *when* the classic decalogue would have acquired its present position it must be said that only a *single* possibility remains open. This must have taken place at some point within the period extending from 622 BC (Josiah's reform) to 560 BC (the composition of the Deuteronomist history which, in the form in which we have it today, clearly presupposes that the decalogue is already in its present place).

[23] E. Gerstenberger (*Wesen und Herkunft des sogenannten apodektischen Rechts*, pp. 83f.) has arrived at the same result, a result to which, moreover, the classic literary criticism is no stranger.

III

THE FORM-CRITICAL PROBLEM OF
THE DECALOGUE

I. APODICTIC LAW IN THE OLD TESTAMENT

As we have indicated in the introduction, the decalogue, seen
through the eyes of a form-critic, belongs to that type of law
which, since 1934, has come to be known among Old Testament scholars as 'apodictic'.[1] Now in order to arrive at a
position from which we can first evaluate and then solve the
form-critical problem of the decalogue we must begin by providing a more detailed account of what the term 'apodictic
laws' is understood to stand for in the Old Testament. Such an
account is all the more desirable in view of the fact that Alt's
definition of apodictic law, which first appeared in 1934, has
since then become the subject of penetrating criticisms both
with regard to the question of what can be considered the
characteristic content of apodictic law and also on the question
of what forms of command and prohibition can probably be
assigned to this category. Since Alt's time two further points
have given rise to discussion concerning apodictic law. On the
one hand the connection between casuistic and apodictic law
has been debated, on the other the question has been raised to
what extent apodictic law would really have been, as a phenomenon, so peculiarly Israelite that no parallels for it can be
found outside the Old Testament. Finally what could be described as a fifth problem—and, moreover, hardly the least
interesting one—is the question of how Israelite apodictic law
is related to a type of literature which is stylistically very close,
namely the exhortations and warnings which play so prominent

[1] See above p. 4.

a part in the Wisdom literature both of the Old Testament and of extra-biblical cultures.

We shall commence our investigation of these questions by briefly delineating certain principal characteristics of apodictic law as defined by Alt. This can best be achieved by following Alt's procedure in giving very briefly the evidence for the casuistic type of law which Israel held in common with the entire cuneiform culture of the Near East, i.e. the Sumerian, ancient Babylonian, Hittite and Assyrian cultures, and presumably the Phoenician-Canaanite culture too.

The first half of the 'Book of the Covenant' (Ex. 21.1-23.9) and Deut. 19-25[2] are dominated by legal statutes which are constructed according to the following basic pattern: 'If a man does such-and-such he shall give such-and-such an amount in compensation (or pay the penalty, or be penalized or be immune from punishment).' The conditional clause, introduced by Hebrew *kī* ('in the event that' or 'if'), provides an exact statement of the hypothetical case (casus), and the concluding clause defines the precise extent of the recompense to be exacted, the penance to be performed or the punishment. The hypothetical case can be still more precisely defined[3] by means of a series of conditional clauses grouped under an opening conditional clause. To introduce these the Hebrew prepositions *'īm* ('supposing' or better 'in the event that') and *we'īm* ('and in the event that' or 'or in the event that') are favoured. Alternatively a generic case may be set at the head of a group in which a series of specific cases may be adduced, after which the degree of compensation, punishment or penance to be exacted is given for the cases in general.[4] Even those whose

[2] Anton Jirku, in particular, has alluded to this. See below, pp. 61ff.

[3] Cf. e.g. Ex. 21.18: 'If (Hebrew *kī*) men quarrel and one strikes the other with a stone or with his fist and the man does not die but keeps his bed, then if (Hebrew *'īm*) the man rises again and walks abroad with his staff, he that struck him shall be clear; only he shall pay for the loss of his time, and shall have him thoroughly healed.'

[4] Cf. e.g. Ex. 21.28-32: 'If an ox gores a man or a woman to death the ox shall be stoned and its flesh shall not be eaten; but the owner of the ox shall be clear. But if the ox has been accustomed to gore in the past, and its owner has been warned but has not kept it in, and it kills a man or a woman, the ox shall be stoned and its owner also shall be put to death.' Following upon this we have a law (v. 30)

acquaintance with the literature of the ancient cultures of the Near East is only slight will immediately recognize this type as familiar. It is to be found in the Sumerian laws,[5] in the Code of Hammurabi,[6] in the Hittite laws[7] and in the ancient Assyrian laws.[8] It is the jurisprudence of these ancient cultures in the strict sense of the word which we find ourselves confronted with here. We have every reason to suppose that in ancient Israel legal decisions were arrived at on the basis of this casuistic law of ancient custom when the elders assembled at the gate in order to hear the case of an accused person and the witnesses to the accusation. In later times, and in regions where legal procedure was sufficiently developed, they would also have heard the defender of the accused.[9]

In the midst of the lists of casuistic laws, however, appear, often in larger or smaller groups, 'legal statutes' of a quite different type. These contain neither a conditional clause in which a general or more specific hypothetical case is stated, nor a concluding clause prescribing the appropriate punishment. Instead a declaration of the law is, so to say, uttered into the world of the Israelites from without. It carries with it a unique

prescribing that when the victim is a boy or a girl (v. 31) or a male or female slave (v. 32) a fine is to be imposed.

[5] In the Code of Lipit-Ishtar from the first half of the 19th century BC. For an introduction and translation cf. S. N. Kramer in *ANET*, pp. 159-161. The Stele of Ur-Nammu, cf. E. Szlechter, 'Le Code d'Ur Nammu', *Revue d'Assyriologie*, 49, 1955, pp. 169-177.

[6] From the 18th century BC; cf. especially Kohler and Peiser: *Hammurabi's Gesetze*, Vol I, 1904, and T. J. Meek in *ANET*, pp. 163-180. From the period immediately preceding Hammurabi's dynasty: The Laws of Eshnunna, cf. A. Goetze in *ANET*, pp. 161-163.

[7] From the 14th century BC; cf. Albrecht Goetze in *ANET*, pp. 188-197; J. Holt, *Kilder til Hittiternes Historie* (Sources for the History of the Hittites), 1951, pp. 216-247.

[8] In their present form from the 12th century BC; cf. T. J. Meek in *ANET*, pp. 180-188; A. G. Lie, *Gamle assyriske Love* (Ancient Assyrian Laws), 1924.

[9] Even in those cases which were brought before the supreme tribunal of the land, before the king himself or those who acted as leaders of a given community it was left to both parties, the plaintiff (witnesses for the plaintiff) and the defendant, to set forth the facts upon which the judges or elders had then to decide. cf. II Sam. 15.1ff. and I Kings 21.8ff. At the time of Zechariah (Zech. 3.1ff.) an office roughly corresponding to that of 'public prosecutor' must have been known. It is possible that there is a reference to a 'defending counsel' in Amos 5.10, where the rich of Samaria are accused of entertaining hatred for *hammōkiaḥ* during the trying of cases 'at the gate'.

authority, often emphasized by the rhythmic form in which its clauses are cast, and, from the form and manner of its presentation, is intended to be fundamental to law as such. In this type of legal statute a series of offences is enumerated to which either simple prohibitions are attached or which are also declared to incur a divine curse. This is the type of legal statute which Alt calls 'apodictic law'. To it he attaches a further group of laws which, although as they appear in modern versions of the Bible they are certainly strongly reminiscent of casuistic law (with an introductory clause in the conditional and a concluding clause laying down the appropriate penalty), are in Hebrew couched in rhythmic form and have a participial construction which takes the place of the 'if' clauses of casuistic law. The penalty laid down in these statutes is normally that of death. Later cursing was introduced as a variation to this. Moreover the statutes appear in series.

We have to reckon then with various subordinate types of apodictic law. The first type, which is strongly represented in the decalogue and elsewhere, is the prohibition (the negative *lō'* with imperfect indicative second person singular), e.g. 'You shall not permit a sorceress to live' (Ex. 22.18). The second type, that of the curse, occurs in Deut. 27.15ff.,[10] where for instance we find: 'Cursed be he who leads a blind man astray' (27.18). The third type which, as it appears, comes very close to casuistic law, is to be found in Ex. 21.12, 15-17 and 22.18, 19. In translation, for instance, Ex. 21.12 reads: 'Whoever strikes a man so that he dies shall be put to death.' Despite its constructional resemblance to casuistic law Alt contends that this statute differs essentially from it, a fact which can be deduced from the form which it takes in Hebrew: *makkē 'iš wāmēt mōt yūmāt*. A series of '*mōt yūmāt*' clauses in Lev. 20.2-27 evinces a certain degree of approximation to the casuistic style. They are introduced throughout by the phrase *'iš 'ªšer*, i.e. 'the man who . . .', and they all end with the declaration of the death penalty, *mōt yūmāt*. According to Alt's conception the characteristics of

---

[10] On the question to what extent the list of curses in Deut. 27 may originally have been a 'decalogue' see above pp. 15ff.

apodictic law can be summed up as follows: 1) The apodictic
laws are fundamental in character. 2) They are radically religious in that it is the divine voice that utters its commands
through them. 3) They are rhythmic and terse in style, and no
superfluous words are used. 4) As a rule they appear in series.
5) In the apodictic laws religion, ethics and law are intimately
interconnected. In style and content alike the apodictic laws
differ from the casuistic ones to the extent that their origin is to
be sought in a quite different context from that in which
casuistic law has its *Sitz im Leben*, for in fact the latter represents
the judgments given at the 'gate'. Now since, as Alt sees it, we
do not encounter any phenomenon corresponding to apodictic
law outside Israel, the latter must be characterized as pertaining to a tradition of law which is peculiar to Israel and is the
outcome of her national religion. 'Everything in them is related exclusively to the Israelite nation and the religion of
Yahweh even where their terse wording does not refer directly
to either.'[11]

With regard to the place of origin of apodictic law Alt is of
the opinion that from all points of view a cultic and ceremonial
context must be indicated. In this connection he can point to
the tradition which draws the particular elements constituting
the framework of Deuteronomy to a conclusion, namely Deut.
31.9-13. Here it is prescribed that every seven years in the year
of release the law is to be read at the feast of Tabernacles so that
the Israelites can learn it and teach their descendants to observe
it. That a ceremony of the sort envisaged by Alt bears a cultic
stamp is to be deduced partly from the connection with the
feast of Tabernacles and partly from the fact that the Levites,
who were the priests of ancient Israel, are made responsible for
handing on the law.

Alt's treatise on the origins of Israelite law has opened up an
extraordinarily fruitful field of research. This was already true
at the outset of the thirty years which have since elapsed, but
perhaps it has been particularly the case since 1953 when the
treatise was republished. But it is easy to allow this to over-

[11] Alt, 'Origins . . .', pp. 111-124.

shadow another factor, namely that long before Alt valuable and stimulating investigations were already being conducted, which Alt took over and developed further in his epoch-making treatise. With regard to the form-critical element in Alt's work he had predecessors in his own pupil, Alfred Jepsen and also in Anton Jirku. Both of these published valuable studies on the Israelite laws in 1927.[12] While Jepsen confined himself principally to the Book of the Covenant, Jirku took as his field of investigation the entire legal material in the Pentateuch, and examined Ex. 20.1-23. 33; 34.10-27; Lev. 17-26; Deut. 5.6-18; 12-26; 27.15-26. He did not include in his considerations the cultic laws of the Priestly tradition, which are to be found in Ex. 25-31; Lev. 1-7; 11-15 and 16. Jirku's original contribution consists in the fact that he defined the different stylistic forms which are used in the collections of laws in the Old Testament.[13] His intention is to show that the smaller collections of laws such as the Book of the Covenant, the Code of Holiness and Deuteronomy (=the fifth book of the Pentateuch) are, in the form in which we have them today, secondary compilations. And he attempts to assemble those laws which exhibit the same style and which therefore probably have the same background also. In the process of being handed down, however, and being subjected to the forces of literary evolution, they have become scattered here and there throughout the Old Testament collections of laws. This author has also anticipated Alt in his observation that of the stylistic forms employed in the Old Testament, only one, the casuistic (Jirku designates it as the 'if' form), has analogies in Sumerian, Akkadian and Hittite legislation. Since the casuistic form is especially prominent in the legislation of Ex. 21-22 and Deut. 19-25, he estimates that both groups once constituted a single whole, a hypothesis which

[12] Anton Jirku, *Das weltliche Recht im Alten Testament*, 1927. Alfred Jepsen, *Untersuchungen zum Bundesbuch*, 1927.

[13] The larger collections, such as the Book of the Covenant, the Code of Holiness and Deuteronomy (Deut. 12-26) are defined as 'books of laws', i.e. compilations of various kinds of legal material which have been handed down and preserved, while two smaller units, the decalogue and the curses in Deut. 27, are called 'codices', i.e. inventories of laws which have been promulgated by a law-giver, drawn up according to an ordered plan. See above p. 52 n. 18.

he considers all the more probable in view of the fact that in terms of content they supplement one another.

Jirku finds ten distinct stylistic forms in all represented in the Old Testament. Certain of these we have already referred to: apart from the casuistic form we have mentioned the categorical prohibition in the second person singular, the curse-formulae of Deut. 27, and the participial formulae of Ex. 21-22. The remaining six types are as follows:

(i) The 'he' formula: 'The man who ... must surely. ...' This is distinguished from casuistic law by its introduction, *'îš 'ašer*, e.g. Lev. 20.10.

(ii) The 'thou shalt' formula, a variation of the categorical prohibition, e.g. Lev. 19.15.

(iii) The 'jussive' formula (which does not necessarily employ the jussive in place of the imperfect); the characteristic mark of this is that the prohibition is expressed in the third person singular or plural, e.g. Deut. 19.15.

(iv) The 'if thou' formula, which is reminiscent of casuistic law, but which differs from it in that it is expressed in the second person singular.

(v) The 'if you' formula corresponds to the last named except that it is expressed in the second person plural.

(vi) Finally the 'double if' formula, which is distinguished from casuistic law only by the fact that the subject of the particular conditional clauses is placed before an introductory 'in the event that' or 'if'. Examples of the last three types are Deut. 22.8; Lev. 19.23; Lev. 24.15.

Having worked out these types Jirku then attempts to establish the characteristics by which the content of each is to be distinguished, and to estimate what degree of antiquity it is possible to ascribe to them. The earliest type is the casuistic law of the Book of the Covenant and Deuteronomy, and in spite of the fact that certain of the laws reflect the life of a community engaged in agriculture we may legitimately deduce that it is in the casuistically formulated laws that we must seek the remnants of the original Mosaic code. The group consisting of categorical commands contains numerous doublets, but within the group many laws are to be found which are undoubtedly very ancient. The content of the remaining groups contains occasional references from which it can be deduced that they reflect a stage in the development of the people which from a sociological point of view is well advanced. Here and there the influence of the prophets can also be discerned. The decalogue, the last of the collections to be treated of in Jirku's book,[14] is regarded as an ethical code which Moses could have assembled from the wealth of material which has come down to us in the Pentateuch as we have it today. Stylistically, however, the individual commandments must originally all have conformed to the same pattern, which is not the case with the existing form of the decalogue.

Jepsen's book differs from Jirku's in that the former attempts to achieve a more systematic grouping of the legal material. The field of his investigations is narrower—it only includes the Book of the Covenant—but his researches are more penetrating. He finds four basic types represented in the Book of the Covenant and, in addition to these, certain mixed forms; these demonstrate their secondary character by their departure from the original stylistic pattern. These four basic forms are:

(i) The Hebrew *mišpāṭīm* (Jirku's 'if' formula, Alt's casuistic law), Ex. 21.2-22.16, where, however, traces of other types do occur.

(ii) The Israelite *mišpāṭīm* (Jirku's 'participial formula', the '*mōt yūmāt*' clauses of Ex. 21 and 22).

(iii) The ethical prohibitions (Ex. 22.27; 23.1-3, 6-9).

(iv) The cultic commandments (Ex. 23.13ff.).

The Hebrew *mišpāṭīm* must have been taken over, so Jepsen considers, by the Israelites after these had established themselves on Canaanite soil. It was not from the Canaanites themselves, however, to whom the horse meant so much (cf. the

[14] *Op. cit.* ch. IX, pp. 150-160.

Hyksos), that they were taken over; for in these *mišpāṭim* we find nothing about horses. It was rather from the Ḥabiru-Hebrews (cf. Ex. 21.2), that they were derived. These appear to have exercised an important function in two cities, namely Shechem and Gibeon, the organization of which was certainly not that of a monarchy. Both these cities came to be connected with the Israelites at the same time, in the period between the entry into the land and the introduction of the monarchy.[15] Jepsen connects the Israelite *mišpāṭim* with the curses of Deut. 27, where the same participial construction predominates. He recognizes a rhythmic style and a religious tone in them, and concludes that the death penalty, or alternatively cursing, suggests a very early date for them. He regards it as possible that we have here remnants of an authentically Mosaic tradition deriving from the wilderness period. The *moral prohibitions* are formulated in the same way as the decalogue, which Jepsen considers to be Mosaic; indeed he regards certain elements in it as actually pre-Mosaic. In these instances, however, a stylistic departure from the old terse formulation is discernible, and it has been noticed that they are on the way to becoming exhortations of the kind that we encounter in the Wisdom literature.[16] The *cultic laws* (Ex. 23.13ff., but also perhaps Ex. 20.23f.) have parallels in Ex. 34. Presumably we have here two series

[15] In connection with Shechem and the Ḥabiru cf. Putu-Ḥepa's Letter to Pharaoh (14th century BC) concerning the handing over of Shechem to the Ḥabiru, Knudtzon, *Die El-Amarna Tafeln*, 1915, pp. 874-75. It is possible that the Hivites who lived in Gibeon constituted a subdivision of the Ḥabiru. It can be deduced from Gen. 34, Judg. 9 and Josh. 9 that the cities referred to were not organized on a monarchical basis when the Israelites first came into contact with them. Jepsen's theory with regard to the Ḥabiru, which entails, amongst other things, the idea of a special connection between the Ḥabiru and the Hivites, cannot be upheld. Although the problem of the Ḥabiru cannot, perhaps, be regarded as definitively solved, almost all the evidence to be found in the history of the Near East in the second millennium BC suggests that the name Ḥabiru stands for a sociological rather than an ethnic group, and that the people so designated are probably best characterized as 'propertyless proletariat'.

[16] Jepsen, *op. cit.*, p. 89. Jepsen is thinking particularly of the 'model for the judge', Ex. 23.1-3, 6-9. He believes that foreign influence may have contributed to the fact that the style began to disappear, but at the same time draws attention to the fact that both the form and content of the axioms in the Book of Proverbs betray a connection with the ancient tradition of Israel. This suggestion of a connection between legal material and Wisdom literature is worthy of close attention.

which go back to the same source, either oral or written. Since they presuppose a peasant culture as already in existence, but have nevertheless been included in the Book of the Covenant, they presumably derive from the period immediately after the entry into the land. *Ḥuqqīm* has presumably become the technical term for these cultic laws, and the ethical commandments would probably have been characterized as *tōrā*.

The difference between Jepsen's and Alt's respective conceptions of the legislation of Israel and its origin can briefly be summed up under the following three heads:

(i) Alt estimates that the casuistic law has been taken over from the Canaanites. ('Hebrew' is not an ethnic but a sociological designation.)

(ii) Alt emphasizes the difference between casuistic law and laws formulated in the participial style more strongly than Jepsen. Jepsen calls these latter Israelite *mišpāṭīm*.

(iii) Alt is of the opinion that the decalogue represents a later stage in the development of apodictic law; this is partly because the decalogue exhibits a conscious tendency to summarize the entire range of apodictic legislation within its short series of ten commandments, and partly because signs of a certain stylistic loosening are apparent in it. On this last point however Alt later modified his position in that he deduced a more primitive form underlying the prohibition of theft. In this primitive form the commandment would have referred only to the theft of men. Here Alt touches upon the question of the primitive form of the decalogue, a question which, of course, entails consequences for the problem of dating.[17]

Alt has met with unreserved agreement especially from K. Rabast, who has produced a study which is compact and rich

[17] Cf. his work 'Das Verbot des Diebstahls im Dekalog' in *Kleine Schriften* I, 1953, pp. 333-340, especially p. 336, where he also refers to (n. 1) Rabast's attempt at reconstructing the decalogue on form-critical principles, but expresses his doubts as to how far Rabast's reconstruction of the original text are satisfactory in all cases. See below pp. 87ff.

in ideas.[18] Here he attempts first to apply Alt's basic approach
to apodictic law to Deuteronomy and the Code of Holiness,
the two legislative compilations which Alt had to leave on one
side because of the plan of his work. In addition to this Rabast
also attempts to develop certain indications of Alt's concerning
the actual stylistic form of apodictic law and concerning the
formation of 'lists', i.e. the fact that the apodictic laws often
appear in shorter or longer lists of commandments and prohibitions. Finally Rabast makes a noteworthy attempt to reconstruct the decalogue from a form-critical standpoint.[19] We
shall return to this attempt later.[20] Here we intend only to show
briefly the manner in which Rabast attempts to develop the
point of view of the master.

With regard to the 'compilation of lists' Rabast distinguishes
between three kinds of lists:

(i) 'Comprehensive lists', which deliberately seek to embrace
the whole range of laws, or to enumerate all the offences to
which the same penalty is attached, e.g. the 'dodecalogue
of curses' in Deut. 27, the '*mōt yūmāt*' commandments,
Ex. 21-22 (this can be supplemented with the list in Lev.
20, where the form is somewhat modified), and finally the
classic decalogue.

(ii) 'Particular lists' which are meant to cover a precisely
defined area of the law. The most striking example here is
Lev. 18.6-18, the rules for sexual behaviour, but the 'model
for the judge' in Ex. 23.1-3, 6-9 can also be adduced.

(iii) 'Short lists.' These are restricted not merely in the sense
that they cover only a small part of the legislation, but
also because they may include only three or four items,
e.g. Deut. 20.5-8: what individuals are not to take part in
military service; Deut. 25.13-16: the 'model for a mer-

---

[18] Karlheinz Rabast, *Das apodiktische Recht im Deuteronomium und im Heiligkeitsgesetz*, 1948. This study is known to me only from a very full summary which the
reviewer, Theologiekandidat Bent Mogensen, most kindly placed at my disposal.
I worked out my own 'reconstruction' of the 'original decalogue' several years
before Rabast, and without any knowledge of his attempt.

[19] *Op. cit.* pp. 35-38.   [20] See below, pp. 87ff.

chant'; and Lev. 19.35-36: prohibition of the use of false weights and measures.

Finally Rabast points out that apodictic laws sometimes appear in isolation, but that in such cases they are often being quoted. With regard to the interrelationship between the three sorts of list Rabast comes to the following conclusion[21]: the 'comprehensive list' represents the earliest stage. Here law and religion are intimately connected, and it can be deduced from the existing context in which the lists appear that they have been preserved and transmitted in a sacral milieu.[22] The 'Particular lists' and 'Short lists', with their specialisation and concentration on special areas of moral and juridical legislation, belong to a later development. To that extent they represent the beginning of a process of secularization which is carried further as casuistic and apodictic laws become progressively fused and combined.

The distinction drawn between the various types of lists is no doubt justified to a certain extent; at any rate it provides a practical working basis. On the other hand, we would contend that any attempt such as Rabast's to arrange the lists in an order of priority must be viewed with a certain scepticism. This is partly because in our opinion it is based upon a preconceived theory of how the relationship between ethics and religion must have developed from earliest times up to the exile, partly because Rabast does not take sufficiently into account the fact that the connection between the 'comprehensive lists' and their existing contexts appears, upon closer analysis

[21] The actual problem of 'compilation of lists' is treated of by Rabast, *op. cit.*, pp. 21-26. On how the three kinds of list are interrelated, and especially on the question of their dating Rabast gives his opinions partly on p. 35—in connection with his attempted reconstruction of the decalogue—partly in the concluding sections on the 'setting in life' of apodictic law, pp. 39ff., and on the sacral character and social orientation of this, pp. 42ff.

[22] Even in what seems to be the most illuminating case, Deut. 27, which for this reason Rabast too has taken as his starting-point (*op. cit.*, p. 39) it may be doubted whether the existing literary connections are original. See above pp. 16f. and further on this my book, *Shechem . . .* , 1955, pp. 50-85, where I have argued that there is a possible connection between the 'dodecalogue of curses' and the ritual of the sealing of the covenant.

from a literary and traditio-historical point of view, as somewhat problematical.[23] The individual analysis of certain 'particular lists' and 'short lists',[24] which has been undertaken both before and after Rabast's work appeared, are also most easily to be explained as pointing in the opposite direction. The same would apply to a radical analysis of the decalogue.

In Rabast's account of the metre, constructions, style and form of apodictic law we find special cause to draw attention to his emphasis on the originally *poetic* form of apodictic law. Wherever this form is weakened by prose elements it is a question of secondary developments, a loosening of the strict stylistic form. He notices also, and rightly, that in those lists in which all the individual clauses must originally have been composed in the same metre both abbreviations and expansions could have been subsequently made. Finally we may notice his contention that the prohibition expressed in the second person singular with *lō'* and the imperfect is the basic form of apodictic law.

A long list of the names of distinguished scholars might be adduced, who have in all essentials associated themselves with Alt's opinions with regard to apodictic law.[25] But here it may be at least equally appropriate briefly to indicate the main lines of the criticism which has been put forward against Alt in recent years, because these criticisms, with their new approach to the problem, also have an essential bearing upon the problem of the decalogue.

In treating of apodictic law Alt had stated that it was 'Israelite in its national affiliations' and 'Yahwist in its divine affiliations'. He had also said that it was especially characteristic of Israel in the midst of the very varied peoples of the Near East. To maintain this is a prerequisite for the 'comparative religion'

[23] On the decalogue see above pp. 44ff.

[24] E.g. that in Lev. 18.7ff. (K. Elliger in *ZAW* 67, 1955, pp. 1-25: 'Das Gesetz Leviticus 18') or the 'Prescriptions for War' in Deut. 20.5ff. (Fr. Schwally, *Der heilige Krieg im alten Israel*, 1901, p. 99; Johannes Pedersen, *Israel*, III-IV, 1940, pp. 9f., cf. also my article, 'La Guerre considérée comme une religion et la Religion comme une guerre', *StTh* 15, 1961, pp. 93-112, especially p. 98).

[25] Noth, von Rad, Zimmerli, R. Bach, Kraus, Würthwein, Beyerlin, Baltzer, Reventlow, to name only a few of the more prominent.

approach, and, in respect of form and content alike, material
has been adduced from Israel's neighbours which shows that
Alt's position must be modified. Already in the first thirty years
of this century Gressmann, the standard-bearer of the German
'history of religions' school, had attempted in his portrayal of
'the earliest legislation of Israel'[26] to distinguish between civil
law (*jus*), which was casuistic in form, and sacral law (*fas*) in
Israel, by the use of stylistic criteria as well as according to
content. He too must be reckoned among Alt's forerunners. But
in comparison with Alt Gressmann shows himself more open
to the idea of foreign influences and the existence of genuine
parallels in the 'pagan' world. The sacral law of Israel is derived
from the instruction of the laity by the priests. Such teaching,
rooted in the cult, and comprising not only instruction but
ethical training as well, is known to us from both Babylonian
and Egyptian documents and also from the literature of Greece.
Reference is made to the Babylonian *Šurpu* lists, a series of in-
cantation tablets which contain lists of sins set out in catecheti-
cal form by the oracle priests: 'Has he done injury to a god,
dishonoured a goddess? Has he dishonoured his father or his
mother? Done injury to his elder sister? Has he used false
weights? Has he accepted unjust recompence? Has he gone into
the house of his neighbour? Has he drawn near to his neighbour's
wife? Has he meddled in sorcery or the conjuring of spirits?'
This is only a representative selection of the various kinds of
sin of which the petitioner may have been guilty, and by which
he may have drawn down the anger of the gods upon himself.
Now he tries to extricate himself from this by sacrifice and
oracles.[27] In form this text is more closely parallel to passages
such as Ezek. 18.5ff. and Pss. 15 and 24, but in content it is
strikingly reminiscent of the precepts of apodictic law. To some
extent this also applies to the Egyptian *Book of the Dead*, which
describes how the dead person recites his 'negative confession'

[26] *Die älteste Geschichtsschreibung und Prophetie Israels*, especially pp. 222-240.

[27] Cf. the translation in Gressmann, *Altorientalische Texte zum Alten Testament*,
2nd ed., 1926, pp. 324f. *Ibid.* pp. 9-12, the translation of extracts from the Egyptian
Book of the Dead. Further on this cf. Galling, *ZAW* 47, 1929, pp. 125-130: 'Der
Beichtspiegel. Eine gattungsgeschichtliche Studie'.

before Osiris and his forty-two judges: 'I have not done that which the god abhors; I have not diminished the cakes offered to the gods; I have not committed adultery, not practised unchastity; I have neither enlarged nor diminished the cornmeasure', etc. The parallelism with Ezek. 18, the prophetic 'examination of conscience', is here direct and palpable.

It was the prohibition expressed in the second person singular however, which constituted the central nucleus of apodictic law. But for this type too parallels from extra-biblical literature are not wanting. In 1954 George F. Mendenhall[28] drew attention to the Hittite documents which belong to the category of 'political treaties' and established the existence of formulae such as e.g. 'Thou shalt not desire any territory of the land of Hatti.'[29] Thereby he sought to prove a point which he intended to take as the point of departure for his theory, namely that the intermingling of casuistic and apodictic laws which we find in the Book of the Covenant has its exact parallels in the treaties of the ancient Near East, and that the Israelites themselves, without any influence from the Canaanites, would have drawn up their Book of the Covenant in conformity with an extremely ancient model, which we find reflected especially in the Hittite treaties. Since it would almost be true to say that Mendenhall's theory of the structure of the covenant formulary[30] has become the tenet of a particular school of thought, the chief points in this formulary must be briefly enumerated here:

(i) The Preamble, introducing the person who is making the covenant (the agreement).

(ii) The Historical Prologue, which describes the course of previous relations between the two partners to the covenant.

[28] In two articles which appeared in *BA* XVII, 2-3, and which were subsequently combined under the title *Law and Covenant in Israel and the Ancient Near East*, 1955. I have reviewed this work at length in *TLZ* 84, 1959, cols. 592-93.

[29] *Op. cit.* p. 7. Form: prohibition in the second person singular; Content: prohibition of coveting, cf. the final commandment of the decalogue, Ex. 20.17.

[30] V. Korosec, *Hethitische Staatsverträge*, 1931, was the originator of this theory. cf. Mendenhall, *op. cit.*, p. 27 n. 10.

(iii) The Covenant Obligations incurred by those who are making the treaty.

(iv) The Prescriptions for the Preservation of the Covenant Document in a sanctuary, and for the periodic reading of it.

(v) The List of the Gods who are invoked as witnesses to it.

(vi) The closing Formulae of cursing and blessing. It is clear that of all the types of 'covenant-making' in the Old Testament, the ones which can be adduced here as possible parallels to the Hittite treaties are not the Abrahamite covenant or the Davidic covenant but the narratives of Moses and Joshua, Ex. 19ff. and Josh. 24. The weak point in Mendenhall's argument is the fact that without closer *literary* analysis he has adduced the decalogue as a covenant document which fits into the plan delineated above, and on these grounds forthwith comes down in favour of the great antiquity of the decalogue and its Mosaic authorship.[31]

It should also be observed that the most recent research has not been willing to recognize all types of legal precepts which Alt includes under the heading 'apodictic' as true apodictic law. H. Gese has proposed in a short article that the designation 'apodictic' should be restricted so as to apply only to prohibitions in the second person singular.[32] These prohibitions are not legal precepts in the true sense, for a precept, a law must include a statement of a given crime and the penalty attached to it. This is what we encounter in the legal material which is casuistically formulated, but also in a form which has undergone poetic variations, and in which the conditional clause has given way to a participial construction. These legal prescriptions are so different from the prohibitions in the second person singular that it is impossible to compare the two types. Casuistic law can lay down legal decisions pertaining to jurisprudence. The apodictic precepts on the contrary belong to the

---

[31] Cf. our discussion of this question above, pp. 44ff.

[32] H. Gese, 'Beobachtungen zum Stil alttestamentlicher Rechtssätze', *TLZ* 85, 1960, cols. 147-150.

cult, or perhaps find a place only in the education of the Israelite man. And this quite different situation explains the fact that the apodictic precepts differ so widely in content from the casuistic ones.[33]

The indications given here are to be found fully worked out as a thesis in a treatise by E. Gerstenberger.[34] This may be regarded as a general attack not only upon Alt's theories of apodictic law but also upon the theory of an original and close connection between apodictic precepts and the 'covenant formulary' of the ancient Near East which we have just described. Here only a few small points will be examined, selected in view of the significance which they may possibly possess for the question of the decalogue as a category.

Having defined the apodictic material as prohibition and command essentially expressed in the second person singular, Gerstenberger examines this material as it occurs in the Book of the Covenant, the Code of Holiness and Deuteronomy, and refers to the decalogue the 'rules of family life' (such as those of the Rechabites, Jer. 35.6), the affirmations of innocence (such as that in Ezek. 18), the '*tora* liturgies', the prophetic threats and the maxims of the Wisdom literature as material which is related to the apodictic precepts and for which he proposes the designation 'prohibitive'. In the nature of things this 'prohibitive' material appears most often in a negative formulation, but Gerstenberger does not consider it necessary radically to impugn the originality of those passages which instead of this exhibit a positive formulation even though in their content they are 'prohibitive' (that one must refrain from some course of action, or, conversely, that one must do something—the command that provides the positive complement to a prohibition; that in such-and-such circumstances man does not need to observe the prohibition, but is equally free to take

[33] The intermingling of apodictically and casuistically formulated clauses such as we meet with in Ex. 21.12ff. should warn us against any exaggerated emphasis on the differences between the *content* of the two types of law. In justice to Gese I must add that he regards the participial constructions in Ex. 21.12ff. as a variant of casuistic law.

[34] The aims of the author are revealed in the very title, *Wesen und Herkunft des sogenannten apodiktischen Rechts im Alten Testament*, 1961.

either of two courses; finally the positive command which has no negative counterpart, e.g. the observance of the Sabbath, the honouring of parents). Even in cases in which the negative formulation predominates in the 'prohibitives', still affirmation and negation belong together in the sense that the avoidance of evil means, in effect, nothing else than the performance of good.[35] Again in the Wisdom literature warnings and exhortations, negative and positive maxims, go hand in hand in precisely the same way. In reaction against any exaggeration of the connection between the warning of Wisdom literature and the 'prohibitive' of apodictic law the objection has bluntly been raised that the 'prohibitives' which, for instance, we encounter in the Book of the Covenant actually have a more intensive character than the maxims of the Wisdom literature, for the former have the grammatical form *lō'* + imperfect, while the latter are formulated in the jussive with the negative *'al*. Gerstenberger seeks to minimize this argument as far as possible,[36] and in any case holds it as an established fact that it cannot be concluded from the '*lō'* + imperfect' construction that the 'prohibitive' so formulated must be supported by divine authority. Moreover prohibitions are to be found which speak of Yahweh or 'God' in the third person, and in such cases the voice which utters the apodictic precepts must indisputably represent a human authority, a law-giver or pedagogue. In terms of content Wisdom literature and 'prohibitive' law are not dissimilar, except for the fact that the 'prohibitive' seem to a large extent to be concerned with cultic and religious matters, while serious crimes of violence do not constitute a central theme in the Wisdom literature.

[35] It must however be mentioned that the passages which Gerstenberger adduces in support of his theory of a connection between the negatively and affirmatively formulated clauses belong exclusively to the later passages, and that the only early passage, Ex. 23.7a is in reality a prohibition. With regard to the elements in the decalogue which are formulated affirmatively see below, pp. 112ff.

[36] *Op. cit.*, pp. 51ff. ('The intensity of the prohibitive'). In reality in summarizing his conclusions, p. 54, he makes many concessions to the traditional view according to which the form *lō'* + imperfect necessarily imparts more authority to a prohibition than a prohibition in the jussive with the negative *'al*, a construction which frequently appears in the later passages in particular.

According to Gerstenberger no one definite 'situation' can be pointed to as the milieu of the 'prohibitive'. There are several possibilities. It can take the form of a 'pattern for officials' or a priestly catalogue having the character of 'canon law', devised, for example, in order to determine who must be excluded from fellowship or from the community. In their more extended form 'prohibitives' may appear in the guise of catalogues of virtues which portray the ideal of the just man—the examples mentioned here are, incidentally, all expressed in the third person singular. Yet the true and basic form of the 'prohibitive' is the prohibition in the second person singular, and the actual mode of formulation implies that the words contained in it are directed to the individual. The rhythmic form is characteristic of these 'prohibitives', and the extremely short formulations which we find in the decalogue cannot be regarded as 'classic' for this category. Furthermore they are almost unrestrictedly general and have too little contact with the concrete world. As a rule the 'prohibitive' must have contained a negation, a verb, an object and subsequently a short account of the immediately relevant circumstances. As an expression of basic moral attitude they are earlier than the development of casuistic law. Jurisprudence decides on the basis of ethical principle that a particular course of action is a crime for which some penalty is laid down.

A further feature of Gerstenberger's study must be mentioned here. With regard to the 'compilation of lists' his views are diametrically opposed to those which we have encountered in Rabast. According to his conception lists of ten or twelve items are the expression of a secondary sytematic theologizing activity. It is the double commandment or the groups of up to three or perhaps four 'prohibitives' which are, so he believes, the original types of 'list'. The area in which these 'prohibitives' would have found their concrete application is that of everyday life, the relationship between a man and his neighbour. The religious commandments, on the other hand (against polytheism, idolatry, misuse of the name of Yahweh, etc.) have their specific origin in the covenant religion of Israel and their connection with the normal 'prohibitives' is revealed, according to Gerstenberger, to be secondary.[37]

The proper place of origin of the 'prohibitive' is instruction in the family circle. They represent 'tribal ethos'. As the passages providing most support for his argument Gerstenberger adduces the Rechabite rule, Jer. 35.6f., the formulation of which is certainly apodictic, and also Lev. 18, a passage which, according to Elliger's analysis, belongs from the outset to the context of the extended family. In addition we have what are, formally speaking, the closest parallels, in the warnings and exhortations of the Wisdom literature, especially in Proverbs 1-9 and 22-24. According to Gerstenberger's conception the absolutely ultimate origin to which these exhortations and warnings can be traced back is one which they have in common with the 'prohibitives' of the Old Testament.

There can, in our opinion, be no doubt that Gerstenberger is in many respects justified in the criticisms which he has advanced, and that by pointing to the 'tribal ethos' he has opened up a new line of research. It is no argument against his thesis to say that at the same time his study has rendered significantly more complex the image which must be formed of the development of Israelite culture. The earlier school of literary criticism considered that the religious tradition which was in existence prior to the period of the 'writing' prophets consisted for the most part of primitive naturalistic or popular religion, and that it was only through the preaching of the prophets that it was elevated to the stage of personal religion. It was only then, so it is believed, that law emerged as the product of this influence of prophetic preaching on popular religion. Contrary to this view Alt decided that both casuistic and apodictic law were present at the very outset of the course of development of Israelite culture, and many have followed in his footsteps in regarding the prophets as directly dependent both on apodictic law itself and on the covenant religion which was connected

---

[37] In this connection Gerstenberger directs a strong but not unjustified attack against the approach in which attempts are made to derive the category of the prohibitive from the covenant formulations, *op. cit.* pp. 80-95.

with it. In both cases it is a clear and comprehensible development that is envisaged. With Gerstenberger the picture becomes
complicated. Historically speaking a basic moral attitude is
present among all the Israelite tribes prior to the point at which
they accepted the religion of Yahweh. Traces of this are to be
found in the 'prohibitives'. It was handed down in the family
circles and was rooted in the semi-nomadic or fully nomadic
culture of the tribes. Yet in principle it is not different from any
other 'family ethos' which we find attested in the history of the
Near East. In the course of the history of the people of Israel
this ethos underwent a process of 'theologization'. It was brought
into connection with the religion of the covenant with Yahweh
and acquired secondary attachments to the juridically moulded
casuistic law in its diverse forms. Apart from this it also followed
a quite different line of development in the milieu of the Wisdom teachers, for we find it expressed in exhortations and
warnings couched in the form of appeals. So long as Gerstenberger confines himself to the broad lines of development in all
this, and does not attempt to determine more precisely the
various stages at which the development took place, his general
conclusion remains valid. Moreover it should have been carried
through to the point at which it could be combined with the
theories from which Gerstenberger so radically disassociates
himself. This would have been achieved if the decisive stages in
the development had been assigned to the period which, so far
as Israelite culture is concerned, antedates all the literary evidence and belongs to the beginning of the history of Israel on
Canaanite soil. But indications are to be found in Gerstenberger's work[38] which point in a less happy direction. The decisive
stages of development are distributed in equal proportions
throughout the entire pre-exilic period of the history of Israel,
and culminate at the beginning of the exile in the Deuteronomist
theology of the covenant. Presumably Gerstenberger intended

---

[38] Cf. e.g. his clinging to the old division in Ex. 24 between an original account
of a covenant meal in vv. 1-2, 9ff. and a secondary tradition, 24.3-8, which has been
attached to this concerning a ceremony of sealing the covenant. The basis of this
would have been the 'covenant document'. A further point is the markedly late
dating of Josh. 24 (p. 93), and the quite arbitrary excision of vv. 25f.

by this to attain to a position in which his theory of a common origin for the apodictic precepts and the exhortations and warnings of the Wisdom literature[39] would achieve probability. But it is precisely the part played by oral tradition in instruction,[40] the very factor which he himself emphasizes more than once, that must make the lateness of the dates suggested for the development here superfluous. In this connection we must be permitted to ask whether an earlier date than that championed by Gerstenberger should, after all, be ascribed to the longer lists of ten or even twelve 'prohibitives', and whether they do not take priority in many cases over double commandments and smaller groups of three or four clauses. A further question indeed is whether it is altogether unthinkable that the process of theologizing attested alike in the Book of the Covenant, the Code of Holiness and also in Deuteronomy—in the two last-named cases certainly under priestly and Levitical influence—can be seen as running parallel to a current flowing in the opposite direction, a process of secularization. The initial point of departure for this would have been the combination of prohibitive and casuistic law, and its further development would have gone together with a social and political development in which control of the great central sanctuaries had the effect, amongst other things, of weakening the connection between the affairs of everyday life and the customs observed at the holy places.[41] One might almost receive the impression that in his view of the development of Israelite culture Gerstenberger, without having actually been explicit on the point, has nevertheless been too dependent upon the general ideas of the older approach of literary criticism. To mention only one concrete example, the Book of the Covenant (Ex. 21.2-23.9) neither

---

[39] In its written form the Wisdom literature is customarily assigned to a date in the later period of the monarchy, and this applies to the earliest sections of the Book of Proverbs.

[40] Cf. *op. cit.*, p. 70, on the capacity of the ancients to learn by heart, and p. 165 (n. 100) on the role of oral tradition in the handing down of the proverbial literature.

[41] In its bearing upon the right of asylum this is shown by Nicolsky, 'Das Asylrecht in Israel', *ZAW* 48, 1930, pp. 146-175. Cf. also von Rad, *Old Testament Theology* I, 1962, p. 56.

refers to nor presupposes the period of the monarchy in Israel.
The entire content of the Book of the Covenant can be explained in terms of the conditions prevailing during the period
of the judges; and this carries us back to the beginning of
Israelite history with, amongst other things, a combination of
casuistic law with 'tribal ethos', all included together in a
covenant context which, in respect of its earliest elements—
Ex. 20.22-26 and Ex. 23.10-19—can most naturally be explained in terms of the situation prevailing in the earliest
period of Israel's history. Perhaps we should add the proviso that
through these words one can catch the sound of a faint protest
against the first manifestations of the period of the monarchy.

Against the background of these considerations we shall
attempt to bring form-critical criteria to bear in the analysis
which follows, the purpose of which is to arrive as far as possible
at a 'primitive form' of the decalogue.

2. AN ATTEMPTED RECONSTRUCTION
OF THE PRIMITIVE DECALOGUE

Before we proceed to present our own conception of what the
original form of the decalogue must have been, three earlier
attempts must very briefly be mentioned at this point.

E. Meier[1] took as his starting-point the idea that the 'prohibition of covetousness' with which the decalogue concludes
is a secondary expansion of the prohibition of theft. In this way
he arrived at the following version of the ten commandments:

First Table	*Second Table*
I, Yahweh, am thy God.	Honour thy father and thy mother.
Thou shalt have no other god besides me.	Thou shalt not commit adultery.
Thou shalt not make any image of a god.	Thou shalt not kill.
Thou shalt not utter the name of Yahweh thy God in falsehood.	Thou shalt not bear false witness against thy neighbour.
Remember the Sabbath day that thou mayest sanctify it.	Thou shalt not steal.

[1] E. Meier, *Die ursprüngliche Form des Dekalogs hergestellt und erklärt*, 1846, pp. 66ff.
The commandments are set out schematically in Hebrew on pp. 76f. (in German
on p. 78).

This theory has the advantage that in this brief collection, in which manifestly the greatest possible number of the basic principles of human life are included, we avoid the necessity of having three commandments before us (the seventh, ninth and tenth according to the Catholic and Lutheran enumerations) in which essentially the same action has been prohibited. It is a disadvantage that the introductory formula of the decalogue is counted as one of the commandments (as in orthodox Judaism). A further disadvantage is that in the midst of the series of prohibitions we find ourselves confronted with the two commandments formulated positively, namely, those referring to the sabbath and honouring parents. Finally it can be said that the attempted reconstruction described here does not satisfy the claims of form-criticism as any such attempt undertaken today must satisfy them.

Hans Schmidt[2] takes as his point of departure the specific idea that the two positive commandments, in virtue of their formulation, represent alien elements in the text as a whole. His attempt at a reconstruction may be set forth as follows:

First Table	*Second Table*
Thou shalt not have any other god besides me.	Thou shalt not kill.
Thou shalt not adore them.	Thou shalt not commit adultery.
Thou shalt not serve them.	Thou shalt not steal.
Thou shalt not make any carved image.	Thou shalt not bear false witness against thy neighbour.
Thou shalt not pronounce the name 'Yahweh' sacrilegiously.	Thou shalt not covet any of the possessions of thy neighbour.

This reconstruction also has its advantages and disadvantages. With regard to the advantages it seems consistent to regard the list of the decalogue as consisting exclusively of negatively formulated commandments. The division between the two tables gives the impression of being at least as appropriate as that of Meier: exclusively religious commandments on the first table, and exclusively ethical ones on the second. Yet

[2] 'Mose und der Dekalog', *Eucharisterion* I, 1923, pp. 78-119: reconstruction of the decalogue on p. 82.

there is no doubt that serious objections can be raised to this attempt of Hans Schmidt's. The very fact that two of the traditional commandments have been struck out without the possibility being considered of whether they may not have existed in negative form provides in itself considerable grounds for reflection. On this point one cannot altogether avoid the suspicion that Schmidt, who comes down strongly in favour of the Mosaic authorship of the decalogue, has felt it as a liberation to rid himself of the sabbath commandment, since in his time those engaged in exploring the question of the sabbath were very strongly of the opinion that the sabbath as a day of weekly religious observance was a product of the late pre-exilic period if not actually of the exile, in other words seven hundred years later than Moses.[3]

A further factor is that the division between 'having strange gods', 'bowing down before them' and 'serving' them cannot fail to strike one as excessively subtle. The intention of the first commandment, it is held, is to prohibit the possession of household gods. The second commandment, is directed against 'bowing down' before a strange god when one comes across it, while what the third commandment is intended to forbid is a deliberate offering of gifts to a strange god. The manner in which the expression 'strange gods' is used in the Old Testament, however, clearly tells against Schmidt's theory to the effect that here it is household gods that are in question. In reality the commandment is directed against any form of polytheism as a matter of general principle, and the force of the ensuing clauses is in reality that of expansions of this principle.

Finally one cannot fail to sense an apologetic tendency in Schmidt when he formulates the tenth commandment as above.

---

[3] J. Meinhold in particular has defended this thesis in *Sabbat und Woche im Alten Testament*, 1905, and 'Die Entstehung des Sabbats', *ZAW* 29, 1909, pp. 81f. and later in *Der Dekalog*, 1927, and 'Zur Sabbathsfrage', *ZAW* 48, 1930, pp. 121-138. The two Danes who have made a deep study of the problem of the sabbath have arrived at the conclusion that the sabbath was celebrated as a weekly day of observance from the earliest period *in Israel*, cf. A. Bentzen, *Den israelitiske Sabbats Oprindelse og Historie* (Origin and History of the Israelite Sabbath), 1923, and P. O. Bostrup, *Den israelitiske Sabbats Oprindelse og Karakter i foreksilsk Tid* (Origin and Character of the Israelite Sabbath in the pre-exilic period), 1923.

The reference to the 'house' has always been a stone of stumbling to those who regard the decalogue as composed by Moses in the course of his promulgation of the law out in the wilderness.

K. Rabast, in a supplement to his work already mentioned,[4] has given his attention to the original form of the decalogue, which was rhythmic in character. In accordance with his basic conception of the 'comprehensive lists'[5] he is compelled to regard the decalogue as extremely ancient, but the present form of it, which is more prosaic than poetic, represents a stone of stumbling for this theory. An additional point of departure for his reconstruction of the decalogue is the consideration that the individual commandments must have existed in more or less the same form, neither excessively long nor excessively short. Now four commandments are composed in a regular rhythmic form consisting of four stresses, namely the prohibition of images, the prohibition of taking the name of Yahweh in vain,[6] that of bearing false witness and finally that of covetousness in the form which is familiar to us from Ex. 20.17a. Taking this as his starting-point, Rabast then arrives at the following original form of the decalogue, or, more correctly, the original dodecalogue, for a hypothesis which he takes into account is that the collection would originally have consisted of twelve clauses.[7]

Introductory formula: I am Yahweh thy God.

1st Commandment: Thou shalt not have any other god before me.

2nd Commandment: Thou shalt not make to thyself any image of a god.

3rd Commandment: Thou shalt not bow down before them.

---

[4] *Das apodiktische Recht im Deuteronomium und im Heiligkeitsgesetz*, 1948, pp. 35-38.

[5] See above, pp. 66f.

[6] The words 'thy God', *'elōhekā*, are rightly regarded as an addition of Deuteronomist inspiration.

[7] In my opinion the reason for Rabast's choice of the unit of twelve is connected with his great respect for Alt's 'Origins of Israelite law', in which the latter refers particularly to Deut. 27.15-26 as an example of the making of 'lists' in apodictic law, and this passage, in the form in which we have it today, is composed as a dodecalogue. The number twelve appears to suggest a connection with the institution of the amphictyony, which Alt regards as the *fons et origo* of apodictic law.

4th Commandment: Thou shalt not pronounce my name sacrilegiously.

5th Commandment: Thou shalt not do any work upon the sabbath.

6th Commandment: Thou shalt not curse thy father or thy mother.

7th Commandment: Thou shalt not kill a man, a person.

8th Commandment: Thou shalt not commit adultery with thy neighbour's wife.

9th Commandment: Thou shalt not steal a man or a woman.

10th Commandment: Thou shalt not bear false witness against thy neighbour.

11th Commandment: Thou shalt not covet thy neighbour's house.

As can be seen there are eleven commandments here and also an introduction, twelve clauses in all which are able to satisfy the demands of form-criticism with regard to similarity of style in the individual clauses.

If this form of the commandments is accepted it is also possible to make a good division of them between the two tables. The introduction together with the first five commandments, which belong to the sphere of religion, should be assigned to one table, and the sixth to the eleventh commandments, which regulate human relationships, should be assigned to the other.

We regard Rabast's attempt at reconstructing the original decalogue as the best which has been made so far, and we recognize his basic principles, namely negative formulation and uniform rhythm throughout the individual clauses, as well adapted to such a reconstruction, but it is precisely for these reasons that we may be permitted here to confine ourselves to certain *critical* observations.

The fact that the introduction is included in the computation of the commandments represents a retrograde step in relation to the attempt of Hans Schmidt. Moreover Rabast's 'twelve' is based upon a crumbling foundation. He adduces Deut. 27.15-26 in support of the view that secondary abbreviations of dodecalogues into decalogues seem often to have occurred. Now the analyses which we have undertaken above seem[8] to demonstrate the opposite, and it is altogether incomprehensible that Rabast should have based himself in this connection on Deut. 27 of all things. A further point which may be raised against Rabast's attempt is that his first true commandment deviates from those which follow in rhythm and style. It contains at least five stresses and the verb is in the third person singular, not the second.[9] In order to fit the third commandment into the stylistic pattern Rabast is further forced to accept a double stressing of the verb for which there is no analogy in the other clauses. With regard to the fourth commandment it is a matter of dispute whether it is justifiable to alter the expression '*šēm Yahweh*' into '*šᵉmî*'.[10] The hypothesis of an originally negative formulation of the sabbath commandment and the commandment to honour parents is understandable even though the negative equivalent for the latter suggested by Rabast may srike one as very unusual. The seventh commandment with its double object, in which two words are placed asyndetically beside each other, appears thoroughly unpleasing from a stylistic point of view, while on the contrary the eighth commandment seems particularly in keeping with the general style. For the ninth commandment too we might suggest a somewhat different formulation but can fully accept the retention of the tenth and eleventh commandments in the form given here.

Instead of entering in greater detail upon a criticism of the reasons which lie behind Rabast's reconstruction in each individual case, we propose to set forth our own suggested reconstruction. The observations which we may have occasion to make in the course of this can at the same time serve as a commentary upon Rabast's suggestion.

[8] Cf. pp. 15ff.

[9] Here again respect for the words of the master can be discerned. cf. Alt, 'Origins . . .' p. 119, n. 100. Hebrew has no verb signifying 'to have'; hence the formula 'There shall not be to you any god besides me', which represents a deviation from the formulation used in the rest of the commandments. It can be tolerated here because this commandment is placed at the beginning of the list.

[10] See our text-critical observations above, p. 37 and also pp. 87f. below.

On the basis of the considerations which we set forth at the beginning of this study it will be clear that we adhere to the number ten as the starting-point for our proposed reconstruction. We do not, however, attach any importance to the more or less even division of the commandments between two tables. We intend wholly to exclude from our analysis the question of the age of the decalogue, and more specifically, the question of whether it will ever be possible to surmise that it derives from Moses. All that we shall permit ourselves to assert as firmly established is the point which we have touched upon at an earlier stage,[11] namely that the form in which the decalogue appears in Ex. 20 seems to be older than the form in Deut. 5, and that it probably established itself at some point between 622 and 560 BC. We shall attempt to discuss the implications of this fact in their bearing upon the age of the original decalogue in the chapters which follow. According to our theory the decalogue in its original form appeared as follows:

First Commandment:	Thou shalt not bow down before any other god.
	lō' tištaḥᵃwwe lᵉ'ēl 'aḥēr
Second Commandment:	Thou shalt not make to thyself any idol.
	lō' taʿᵃśe lᵉkā pesel
Third Commandment:	Thou shalt not take the name of Yahweh in vain.
	lō' tiśśā' 'et-šēm Yahwe lᵉšāw'
Fourth Commandment:	Thou shalt not do any work on the sabbath day.
	lō' taʿᵃśe mᵉlā'kā bᵉyōm haššabbāt
Fifth Commandment:	Thou shalt not despise thy father or thy mother.
	lō' taqle 'et-'ābīka wᵉ'et-'immeka
Sixth Commandment:	Thou shalt not commit adultery with thy neighbour's wife.
	lō' tin'ap 'et-'ēšet rēʿekā

[11] Cf. p. 43 and p. 55.

Seventh Commandment: Thou shalt not pour out the blood of thy neighbour.
lōʾ tišpōk ʾet-dām rēʿekā

Eighth Commandment: Thou shalt not steal any man from thy neighbour.
lōʾ tignōb ʾiš mērēʿekā

Ninth Commandment: Thou shalt not bear false witness against thy neighbour
lōʾ taʿane bᵉrēʿekā ʿēd šaqer

Tenth Commandment: Thou shalt not covet thy neighbour's house.
lōʾ taḥmōd bēt rēʿekā

In the form which appears here all the commandments have this in common, that they refer to some concrete object and are quite unambiguous. Moreover, taken as a collection, they have the character of basic principles, and the fact that they all uniformly exhibit the same apodictic construction lends emphasis to this. The use of the second person singular together with the negative *lōʾ* in this apodictic form gives the collection a uniquely authoritative tone. In the commandments as reconstructed here no violation of Hebrew style or syntax is to be found, and in all of them the speaker is the law-giver, not Yahweh himself. It is the *law*-giver who speaks, for in content the prescriptions go far beyond the exhortations of the father of a family or a Wisdom teacher addressing immature youths. This collection is addressed to the *adult* Israelite. This appears not least from the last five commandments in which the phrase 'thy neighbour' occurs. It also applies to the prohibition of showing dishonour to parents. The full meaning behind this simple commandment is that those who are in the prime of life must not neglect to care for the older generation. It is true that formally speaking the commandments can be divided into two groups, one in which the expression 'thy neighbour' appears, another in which it is not used; but this should not be allowed to obscure the fact that the commandments cover three main spheres:, first the sphere of cult and religion (1-4); secondly, respect for the life and well-being of others in one's immediate environment (5-7); and thirdly, respect for the rights of others as members of the larger social group (8-10). This division, however, may appear excessively theoretical in that it is difficult to draw the dividing line between the second and third groups.

In the sections which follow we shall attempt very briefly to give our reasons for holding that each of the commandments should be reconstructed in the manner set forth above. We have no intention of providing an exhaustive exegetical study of the commandments, but in the chapter which follows, in which we shall be treating of the traditio-historical problem of the decalogue, we shall attempt to trace the decalogue's course of development from what is here taken to be its original form to the final form which it assumes in Ex. 20 and Deut. 5. In order to avoid misunderstandings we must emphasize at this point that this entire work must in the nature of things be strongly hypothetical in character, but without working hypotheses there can be no progress whatever in research into the decalogue.

Introduction, Ex. 20.2

In our reconstruction we have decided to omit the introduction altogether from our consideration. The reason for this is that the introduction, in so far as it can be retained as authentic, turns the entire decalogue into an address by Yahweh; yet this is contradicted by the third commandment, at any rate in the form in which it has come down to us. It is true that in the prophetic passages of the Old Testament we do find very frequently an alternation between the divine 'I' and 'Yahweh' as referring to God in the third person; but in such passages it is a totally different literary category that is in question. Behind this usage lies the prophet's consciousness of vocation, his experiences of an ecstatic kind and his desire to make his prophetic preaching as clear and unmistakable as possible.

First Commandment, cf. Ex. 20.3 and 34.14

Form-critical considerations have led us to prefer the formulation of Ex. 34.14, in which it is polytheism that is forbidden. One might, with Rabast,[12] also invoke Ps. 81.9, which does have some kind of connection with the basic commandment of the decalogue, and in which, in place of the plural form *'elōhīm 'ᵃḥērīm*, 'other gods', we find the form *'ēl zār*, 'a strange god', and in the parallel hemistich *'ēl nēkār*, 'a foreign god'. It would be possible, moreover, to take the entire sentence in v. 9b as an alternative to the reconstruction which we have proposed (taken from Ex. 34.14), inasmuch as the usage *'elōhē hannēkār*, 'the strange gods' can undeniably be traced further back in Old Testament tradition than the expression *'elōhīm 'ᵃḥērīm*, 'other gods'.[13] But it is hardly possible to arrive at a firm decision as to whether the original words were *'ēl 'ᵃḥēr* or *'ēl nēkār*. On form-critical grounds we prefer the verb *hištaḥᵃwwā* because by employing this verb we can formulate the first commandment in the second person singular. Besides this point, the verb appears in the secondary additions to the first two commandments.

Second Commandment, Ex. 20.4a

The fact that the opening section of v. 4 is to be counted as belonging to the original decalogue is so generally accepted by all those who believe at all that the decalogue had a more primitive form, that there is no need to expend further words upon it.

Third Commandment, Ex. 20.7a

The clause in which the motive underlying this commandment is expressed represents a valuable commentary upon it in its own right, but on form-critical grounds must be excised. Again the addition of the phrase *'ᵉlōhekā*, 'thy God', after

---

[12] *Op. cit.*, p. 36.
[13] On all these questions cf. my works, *Shechem*, 1955, pp. 101-105 and 'The Burial of the Foreign Gods', *StTh* 8, 1954, pp. 103-122.

'Yahweh' overloads the metre and must likewise be excised. The addition presupposes that this commandment was not formulated as an address of Yahweh ('my name') at the time that it was inserted, but rather that Yahweh was spoken of in the third person ('the name of Yahweh'). It must be allowed however that the form *'et-šēm Yahwe* could be derived from an ancient scribal error. Judg. 19.18 would provide a clear analogy for this. According to the existing text of this passage the Levite declares that he is on the way to Yahweh's house, *bēt-Yahwe*, whereas the original text (see Judg. 19.29) undoubtedly read *'my* house'. A copyist has taken the '-*i*' as an abbreviation of the divine name. The solution of this question has far-reaching consequences for the understanding of the decalogue. If we 'correct' *'et-šēm Yahwe* to *'et-šᵉmī* the decalogue *as a whole* appears as an address of Yahweh, and in that case the objection that is validly raised against this, that the introductory formula should not be regarded as an integral element in the decalogue, loses its force. On this view, as we shall see later,[14] the decalogue becomes attached to a particular situation which is altogether different from that which we must envisage as the background to it, considered as the utterance of the law-giver. Rhythmic considerations might be adduced which appear to tell in favour of altering the text to *'et-šᵉmī*, but the ninth commandment shows that the slightly longer form still fits into the framework of the decalogue.

Fourth Commandment, Ex. 20.10a

We have been led by form-critical arguments to choose the negative formulation, the more so because it is to be found in a text which, in its present form, has undergone so much expansion (see above on the first commandment). Our reason for adding a *bᵉyōm*, 'on the ... day' before the word *šabbāt* is the fact that the usage *baššabbāt*, which would otherwise immediately recommend itself by reason of its shorter form (cf. Rabast) is not attested before Nehemiah (10.32; 13.15, 16, 21), while on the contrary the form which has been preferred here also

---

[14] See below pp. 128ff.

appears, apart from this passage (in v. 8), in Ex. 31.14 and in the extremely early passage of 35.3. A *kol* (in this context 'any ... whatever') before *mᵉlā'kā*, 'work' (cf. 31.14) would be worth considering in view of v. 10, but in our passages it often represents what might be called a liturgically strengthening element.

Fifth Commandment, Ex. 20.12a, cf. Deut. 27.16

From among the negative formulations of apodictic law[15] which have come down to us we have chosen a combination of negative + the verb *qālā*, 'to despise', as the expression with the greatest range of meaning. This can better express the negative equivalent to the existing positive formulation than the verb *hikkā*, 'to strike' (cf. Ex. 21.15) or *qillēl*, 'to curse' (cf. Ex. 21.17). The two last-named possibilities do admittedly seem more concrete in their content than the one which we have actually chosen. But as we shall shortly see, in the case of the decalogue, it does not necessarily follow that the most concrete expression of all must also be regarded as the most original. As Alt has pointed out,[16] the decalogue represents an attempt to summarize the greatest possible number of precepts from the sphere of apodictic law in the shortest possible compass. That v. 12b must be regarded as subsequent filling out is self-evident.

Sixth Commandment, Ex. 20.14, cf. Lev. 20.10

We have now arrived at the three short commandments, which even Gerstenberger feels the need to complete.[17] For this sixth commandment we can adopt Rabast's reconstruction, this being identical with the one which we ourselves would suggest.

Seventh Commandment, Ex. 20.13, cf. Gen. 9.6; Jer. 7.6; 22.3

In the reconstruction proposed by Rabast the verb in our passage, Ex. 20.13 is retained as it is found in the existing text.

---

[15] Taking the expression in the broader sense here as in Alt, 'Origins ...'.

[16] *Op. cit.*, pp. 312f.

[17] Gerstenberger, *Wesen und Herkunft* ..., pp. 67f.

We have already expressed our criticisms of this view in the course of describing Rabast's theory. Now since we find the word *rēʿekā* occurring in the sixth, and the eighth to the tenth commandments, at any rate in the form suggested by us, we have form-critical grounds for holding that the seventh commandment too once contained this word *rēʿeka*. However a sentence such as *lōʾ tirsaḥ ʾet-rēʿeka*, 'Thou shalt not kill thy neighbour', gives the impression of being too short to be rhythmical. Now two passages in the temple sermon of Jeremiah, in the form in which we have it today in Jer. 7, contain allusions to the decalogue. The best known is the passage in v. 9, which is reminiscent of Hos. 4.2, and which, like the passage in Hosea, presupposes a text which is reminiscent of Ex. 20.13, 14, 15. At the same time in Jer. 7.6 we meet with allusions to apodictic law, some of them to the decalogue itself. Their style is that of preaching, and they are formulated in the second person plural: 'You shall not oppress the alien, the fatherless or the widow; you shall not shed innocent blood in this place; you shall not go after other gods to your own hurt.' In the collection of 'oracles for the king' in Jer. 21-23 we come across similar allusions to apodictic law (22.3), here directed against some personage or personages who, according to the ideas prevalent in the ancient Near East, were responsible in a special degree for maintaining moral behaviour among the people, namely the kings. In both passages the oracles of Jeremiah have undergone a process of slight alteration owing to the Deuteronomist outlook of those who handed them down, and were responsible for large sections of the Book of Jeremiah. In Gen. 9.6, a verse which belongs to the Priestly strand of tradition in the Tetrateuch, the prohibition of shedding 'the blood of man' is rhythmically formulated, brought into connection with the Priestly Creation narrative, and presented as a law possessing universal force. There can be no real doubt that the turn of phrase used here belongs to the realm of apodictic law. In the reconstruction which we have proposed here it acquires a content which is quite concrete and precise by being connected with *rēʿekā*. It expresses a prohibition of homicide committed in private. We shall go into the reasons for the changing of *šāpak dām* into *rāṣaḥ* at a later stage.

Eighth Commandment, Ex. 20.15, cf. Ex. 21.16

The reconstruction given here is the outcome of generally held form-critical views, and is based upon a theory which Alt[18] in particular has shown to be valid: if the final commandment of the decalogue really was a prohibition of seizing the property of another, then in this short list of ten commandments it would violate every principle of economy, i.e. it would be wholly irrational to use two differently formulated precepts to say the same thing. In other words the prohibition of theft which, in its existing form, is formulated very briefly, requires an object; and this object cannot be identical with the object of the verb 'to covet' in v. 17a, or with the expansion of this in v. 17b ('your neighbour's wife, or his manservant, or his maid-servant, or his ox, or his ass, or anything that is your neigh-bour's'). As Alt has pointed out, the list in v. 17b (which is secondary) of the circle of those normally presided over by the father of the family omits one member, namely the Israelite free man. We find the prohibition of stealing him in the apodictic law,[19] and that in a form in which it is also made clear that the offender will surely incur the death-penalty, whether he has kept the stolen man for himself or sold him as a slave (Ex. 21.16). It is precisely because in the enumeration of 20.17b we have a prohibition of appropriating one's neighbour's wife, but none of appropriating the free men who belong to his family circle, that we cannot concede that the reconstruction proposed by Rabast, 'Thou shalt not steal a man or a woman', *lō' tignōb 'īš wᵉ'iššā*, is justified.

Ninth Commandment, Ex. 20.16

This commandment has manifestly been preserved in its original form. On the question of whether the form in Exodus, *'ēd šāqer*, 'false witness for the prosecution', or that found in

---

[18] Cf. his article 'Das Verbot des Diebstahls im Dekalog', *Kleine Schriften* I, 1953, pp. 334, 339.   [19] Cf. p. 89, n. 15.

Deuteronomy, '*ēd šāw*, 'base witness' is original see above chapter II, p. 42.

Tenth Commandment, Ex. 20.17a

To the considerations put forward in chapter II concerning the content of this commandment we may add a further point to which Alt[20] has drawn attention: the word *ḥāmad*, which we translate 'covet', appears in the inscriptions of King Azitawadda of Karatepe with the word 'city' as its object, A III 14 and C IV 16: 'But if any king from among the kings or prince from among the princes, if a man who is a leading man resolves to efface the name of Azitawadda from this memorial stone of the gods and to set (another) name (upon it), if he actually *y-ḥ-m-d* this city and says . . .' etc. (C III 13-17).[21]

Our form-critical investigation of the decalogue will only be complete when we have succeeded in arriving at a fully satisfying answer to the question 'To what sort of 'setting in life' would such a collection of apodictic laws, ethical commandments and prohibitions have been appropriate?', or, to put it another way, when we have succeeded in giving an adequate explanation of why these ten commandments have been assembled in what is here presumed to be their basic form. From the observations which we have made above it will be clear that the answer to this question must, to a very large extent, be connected with two further questions, first 'What must the original form of the third commandment have been?' and second, 'How should we decide whether the introductory formula did or did not belong to the decalogue in its original form?' We consider it expedient, however, to postpone this difficult question yet a little longer. We are convinced that an analysis of the style and content of the present text of the decalogue, together with an examination of a series of relevant Old Testament texts, will place us in a position to give an outline of the history of the decalogue tradition. We must therefore attempt

---

[20] 'Das Verbot des Diebstahls . . .' p. 334 n. 1.
[21] Text according to Donner and Röllig, *Kanaanäische und aramäische Inschriften*, 1962, p. 6. (Cf. *ANET*, p. 500. Tr.)

such an outline before going on to decide this final question concerning the decalogue's original 'setting in life'. For it may well be that it is in this history of the decalogue tradition that we shall find a pointer indicating where the most reasonable solution lies, when the time finally comes to decide the question.

IV

THE TRADITIO-HISTORICAL PROBLEM
OF THE DECALOGUE

I. INTRODUCTION

WHEN someone has the history of a people, a city, a subject or a text to record it is well worth while to begin with the earliest evidence available with regard to the people, city, subject or text concerned, and to make sure that within this evidence the point at which he chooses to start really is the beginning. His aim is from this point to portray the development stage by stage until he reaches that particular point which he has himself chosen as his conclusion.

This principle must now be applied to the history of the decalogue tradition. It would be possible to begin with the original form as reconstructed above, and then attempt to give a picture of the subsequent fate of this document. The work which this would entail would consist of a more exact analysis of the abbreviations, expansions and modifications which the original document has undergone, in order to arrive at the present form of the decalogue, in other words to deduce the history of the decalogue from the alterations to which it has been subjected.

There is, however, *one* basic obstacle which prevents us from embarking forthwith on such a course. As has been emphasized above our reconstruction of the original decalogue is to be regarded only as a working hypothesis. There is not a single point at which the results yielded by form-critical research have been assured—in so far as one can speak of sureness in this context at all. It might appear more justifiable to proceed in the opposite direction, from the existing form of the decalogue back to what is presumed to have been its original form. Such a procedure would to a certain extent be in conformity with the work of form-criticism which we have done in the previous chapter, only with the difference that whereas in the form-critical analysis we spared no pains in our effort to abstract from the historical development, in a traditio-historical presentation it is precisely this question of historical development which would have to constitute the focal point. Such a procedure of 'working backwards', however, would involve a whole series of doubtful factors. How could we undertake it without first having before us a detailed plan of the development of Israelite and Jewish culture? Moreover, since in our historical thinking our minds are so wholly habituated to conceiving of a development as proceeding from its beginning to its end and not *vice versa*, this way of conceiving of the traditio-historical problem could very easily turn out to be more confusing than enlightening.

There remains a third solution: to carry out the traditio-historical analysis in such a way that we treat first of the secondary expansions, then of the secondary abbreviations, and finally of the transformation of two of the negative prohibitions into positive commandments. The results of such an analysis can then be assembled in a traditio-historical sketch, by means of which the development of the decalogue can be traced from the original form as we have reconstituted it to the form in which we have it today in Ex. 20 and Deut. 5. On this basis the final, but by no means the least important question can be put, one which is important both for the problem of the age of the decalogue and for that of its original 'setting in life'. This is the question of whether the decalogue would have been presented from the outset as Yahweh's direct speech with an introduction which defines it clearly as a covenant 'deed', or whether it would have represented a collection of laws the special 'setting in life' of which we would then have to attempt to determine more closely.

2. THE SECONDARY EXPANSIONS OF THE DECALOGUE

Five commandments of the decalogue have clearly under-gone secondary expansions: the prohibition of images (or per-haps better, the prohibition of praying to other gods including the prohibition of images), the prohibition of misusing Yah-weh's name, the sabbath commandment, the commandment to honour parents and the prohibition of covetousness.

The Expansions of the Law against Images, Ex. 20.4b-6

When we were discussing the problem of the enumeration of the commandments in the decalogue[1] we noticed the peculiar structure apparent in vv. 3-6: a law against images (v. 4) inserted into one against 'having other gods' (v. 3) and honour-ing them (v. 5a). The motive adduced for this is the exclusive character of Yahweh (vv. 5b-6). In their present form these verses must be interpreted as follows: Israel may not honour any other gods besides Yahweh, but Israel may not even honour Yahweh by showing honour to a divine image intended to be a representation of anything whatsoever in the universe more or less symbolical of Yahweh. Yahweh will not tolerate any such divine image in Israel, even when it is thought of as a symbol of himself. Yahweh will actually be jealous of his own image, and will punish Israel for any such apostasy even to the third and fourth generation. If, however, we bear in mind the structure mentioned above we shall recognize that the real object of Yahweh's jealousy is Israel, because of the apostasy which she may commit, whereas the prohibition of images is presented without any special motivation, only with an emphatic rejection of any symbolic representation of Yahweh in the form of any living thing whatsoever. The questions need-ing to be answered at this stage are the following: (1) Are all the expansions which we establish in vv. 3-6 of the same kind, or do they betray different interests? (2) How and why has the law against images come to be inserted into the one against 'having strange gods'? (3) Is there any connection between this

[1] See pp. 10ff. above.

insertion about images and the altered formulation of the first commandment of the decalogue?

(1) The expansions are not all on the same level. To begin with the expansion of the law against images—this, with its systematic division of the universe into three parts, heaven, earth and water, betrays an ideological connection with Gen. 1.20-28, and, moreover, has one further point in common with Gen. 1, the idea of the image of God. In the creation narrative man is described as having been created in God's 'image' (*ṣelem*, in the Old Testament and in the culture of the ancient Near East often having the concrete force of 'statue'), and also in his 'likeness' (*dᵉmūt*, 'abstract representation' from *dāmā*, 'to resemble'). Here, in the forbidding of images, man is not singled out for special mention but the original prohibition of a *pesel*, a 'carved image', is explained as forbidding any conscious attempt at setting up a figure (*temūnā*) which is intended to represent some living creature in the universe. Any idea that the expansion of the law against images is dependent from the literary point of view on the Creation narrative in Gen. 1 is wholly improbable. It would be easier to suppose that the author of Gen. 1 consciously avoided the word *temūnā* because he knew the law against images in its existing form. As to the date of this expansion, all that can be stated firmly is that its image of the world is that of the land after the settlement as known to us from the temple psalms of the Old Testament, the language of which, moreover, is permeated with Canaanite borrowings. We have only to read festal psalms such as Ps. 24 (the entry of the ark of the covenant into Zion; the Lord of the heavenly hosts has founded the earth upon the streams), and Ps. 29 (the voice of Yahweh in heaven resounds over earth and water alike). The prohibition of images itself, on the contrary is directly opposed to the traditions of the land after the settlement to such an extent that the simplest explanation of it is to be found in the well-known dislike of dressed stones[2] in nomadic

---

[2] Cf. G. Beer, *Steinverehrung bei den Israeliten*, 1921. See the law of the altar, Ex. 20.24f., and the instructions for the building of the altar, Deut. 27.5-7, and my work, *Shechem . . .* 1955, pp. 59f.

and Bedouin cultures. This dislike too is based on religious grounds.

(2) The law forbidding images is now inserted into the one against having strange gods, vv. 3, 5a, 5b-6. We can imagine how this would have taken place in detail if we compare the two commandments in the original form which we have reconstructed (A) with the commandments in their existing formulation (B).

A	B
Thou shalt not bow down before any other god	Thou shalt have no *other gods* before me.
Thou shalt not make to thyself any divine image	*Thou shalt not make to thyself any divine image* (any likeness whatsoever . . .)
	Thou shalt not bow down before them or honour them, for I, Yahweh thy God am a jealous God, who visits the sins of the fathers on the children to the third and the fourth generation of those who hate me, etc.

First the prohibition of idolatry which, as originally formulated, was quite concrete in conception has been transformed into a general principle and has been given greater emphasis by means of the expanded formulation. In all this, in respect alike of subject-matter, style and language we can discern the influence of the movement which, politically speaking, culminated in Josiah's reform, and from the point of view of literature culminated in the completion of the Deuteronomist history. This applies, as has long been realized, to the expression 'other gods', the combination of the verbs *hištaḥᵃwwa*, 'to bow down before' and *'ābad*, 'to serve or honour', and possibly too to the addition of *'ᵉlōhekā*, 'your God' after 'Yahweh' in the clause giving the reason. The use of the expression *'al-pānāy*, 'before my countenance' or possibly 'against my countenance' clearly bears the stamp of the tradition of the temple at Jerusalem, where the expression 'Yahweh's countenance' has a vital significance as an expression of his presence in the temple.[3] In other words, the Deuteronomist movement, rooted as it is in a tradition different from that of the temple circles at Jerusalem, and elements of which go back to Northern Israelite circles,[4] has here been combined with the tradition of the temple of Jerusalem, and the transformation of the first commandment is the outcome of this fusion. Thus the original form of the first commandment has been pushed out of place to make way for a new formulation more in conformity with the views of particular circles and particular periods. Finally the reason given in vv. 5b-6 represents an extremely ancient and genuinely Israelite element, which represents Yahweh as the 'jealous' God, an element which here appears in combination with the sharp cleavage drawn by the Deuteronomists between those who are sinful and hate God and those who keep his commandments and love him. We have already spoken[5] of the dependence, so far as the formulation is concerned, upon the passage in Ex. 34.7f.

If, then, it is the case that the law against images has been inserted into this complex with the result that it now divides what must once have been united, the reason can only be that it was desired to attach the same importance to forbidding images of Yahweh as to forbidding idolatry. It is the same tendency which we encounter in the history of the golden calf (Ex. 32),[6] and among the prophets Hosea, who exercised his ministry in the northern kingdom about 730-720 BC, is the earliest representative of this tendency. Viewed in broader perspective what we are encountering here is that anti-Canaanite reaction which appears as one of the decisive factors in the

[3] Cf. especially the Psalms (4.6; 16.11; 17.15; 21.6, 9; 24.6; 27.8, etc.) and those sections of the Priestly writing in Exodus and Numbers which appear in this respect to reflect the cult of Jerusalem.

[4] Cf. e.g. G. von Rad, 'The form-critical Problem of the Hexateuch', pp. 36ff.; Alt, 'Die Heimat des Deuteronomiums', *Kleine Schriften* II, 1953, pp. 289-305; my work, *Shechem*, 1955, pp. 39-85; 298-300; 316f.; 334f.; 339-342.

[5] See p. 36 above.

[6] See p. 32 n. 12 above. While this does represent a form of the cult of Yahweh, nonetheless, since it constitutes a clear breach of the covenant, it is condemned as religious apostasy.

history of the kingdom of Judah in the seventh century BC. Here
it comes to be combined with the impulse towards national
freedom which attacks all forms of Assyrian influence and
which, during the brief period between 622 (Josiah's reform)
and 609 (Josiah's death at the battle of Megiddo) becomes the
official policy of the Jewish state.

(3) In the form in which we have them today vv. 3-6 are
formulated in the style of Yahweh's direct speech. We have
here the expressions *'al-pānāy*, 'before my countenance' (v. 3),
'anōkī Yahweh, 'I Yahweh' and *lᵉśonᵉʾāy*, 'of those who hate me'
(v. 5), *lᵉʾohᵃbay* 'of those who love me' and *miṣwotāy* (v. 6). This
formulation in the first person singular does not, however,
necessarily belong to the transformation of the original prohibitions of idolatry and of images. As the connection with Ex.
34.7f. shows, this transformation could perfectly well have been
achieved if Yahweh had been spoken of in the third person
singular: 'Thou shalt not have other gods before Yahweh's
countenance . . . for Yahweh thy God is a jealous God, visiting
. . . upon . . . those who hate, and showing mercy to . . . those
who love him and keep his commandments.' The alterations
which are necessary in order to change this form into that of
the first person are very slight: the removal of the 'Yahweh'
in v. 3, the addition of an *'anoki*, 'I' in v. 5, and in three places
the excision of the letter *waw* in the suffixes in vv. 5-6. There
need have been no connection, therefore, between the insertion
of the prohibition of images and the subsequent transformation
of the sentence from the third into the first person singular.

Expansion of the Law against the Misuse of Yahweh's Name, Ex. 20.7

The expansions here consist partly in the addition of the word
'eloheka after Yahweh's name in v. 7a, and partly in the final
clause giving the reason: 'For Yahweh will not hold him guilt-
less who takes his name in vain.' The first addition is wholly in
the spirit and style of the Deuteronomists. The second, which
contains a repetition of the commandment in the relative
clause, may be nothing more than an ancient commentary on
the commandment making clear its underlying aim. This

would have been that those who are justly accused of a crime should not make a declaration upon oath of their innocence so as to gain an acquittal, hoping that thus in the 'sacral ordeal' following upon the oath they would be held just.[7] As an introduction to this interpretation of the prohibition cf. Ps. 24.4 (*qerē*). Anyone acting in this manner has brought the holy name of Yahweh into the sphere of lying and deceit, and thereby he can only draw down upon himself the curse. It is possible that a certain connection with the ninth commandment of the decalogue is also to be discerned. But in the ninth commandment it is a question of false accusations in a legal trial, whereas what is envisaged here is rather a false defence offered in the course of a sacral ceremony. For all this it must be allowed that the possibility does remain that the real significance of the expansion of the third commandment is that it circumscribes the area covered by this commandment. In its simple basic form the prohibition could very well have been quite general in character, being directed against all possible kinds of connection between the religion of Yahweh and the superstition and magic prevalent among the people. Just such a confrontation is attested for a period as early as the kingdom of Saul, and is connected with the fact that the religion of Yahweh was radically different from the cult of the dead, conjuring of spirits, the interpretation of dreams, ancestor worship, etc.

Expansion of the Sabbath Commandment, Ex. 20.8-11

At this point we shall confine ourselves to treating of the expansion in the form in which we find it in Ex. 20.[8] We have already discussed its relationship to the conclusion of the Creation narrative in Gen. 2.1-4a, and have pointed out that it is impossible to assert that Ex. 20 shows a literary dependence upon Genesis.[9] What is most vital here is the motivating clause

[7] For a single example of such a divine judgment cf. Num. 5.11ff. Cf. also for instance Ps. 7 and Job 31.

[8] On the variant Deuteronomist form of the clause giving the reason see above pp. 39ff.

[9] The fact that as far as the sabbath commandment is concerned Ex. 20 is not dependent upon Gen. 1 is wholly in accordance with the result at which we arrived with regard to the law against images, see above p. 97.

in v. 11, on which we propose to reserve judgment for the present.

When our reconstruction of the original formulation of the sabbath commandment is compared with the form in which it appears in vv. 8-10, two points are immediately striking: first, that some element of the original formulation survives but has been thrust into the background,[10] second that the character of the sabbath as a day of religious observance, i.e. a festival day, is strongly marked. There is a difference between a festival day and a 'taboo' day. A taboo day is one on which such and such a course of action is forbidden for such and such persons. Now in its original formulation the sabbath appears as an absolute taboo day. A festival day on the contrary is a day on which a new reason is provided for resting from toil, namely that on the day in question a 'positive' cultic action must be performed. It would take us too far afield to try to trace the 'advent and development' of the sabbath in Israelite culture, or to discuss the possibility that it may originally have been connected with the phases of the moon and the Babylonian *šapattu* day.[11] We confess ourselves to be followers of the thesis put forward by Eerdmans and Budde, according to which the sabbath in prehistoric times was a taboo day observed among the tribe of the Kenites, which consisted essentially of smiths, the original sabbath law consisting of a ban on lighting fires (Ex. 35.3, cf. Num. 15.32ff., where the exaction of the death penalty is described in the case of a man who had collected wood on a sabbath). The Israelite tribes, who had cult practices in common with the Kenites, took over this taboo day from them. This may explain both the prominent place occupied by the sabbath law in the decalogue and also its originally nega-

[10] Cf. the fact that this is once more in agreement with the treatment of the first and second commandment.

[11] As has been mentioned in n. 3 on p. 80 above, two excellent treatments of the sabbath are available in Danish: those of A. Bentzen and P. O. Bostrup. Both authors maintain that regardless of what the sabbath may have been at an earlier stage, as early as the pre-Israelite period it had already become identified with the seventh day, and that in the course of the history of Israel it altered its character and, from being a taboo-day alone, became at the same time a festival day.

tive form.[12] In the period of the kings, as is well known, we
encounter the sabbath both as a taboo day and as a festival day,
and both aspects continue to survive in Judaism to the present
day.[13] It is clear that the new form of the sabbath commandment, positive instead of negative, is closely connected with the
change of the sabbath from being a taboo day to being a festival
day as well. The precise point at which such a change would
have taken place is hardly possible to determine, but it appears
to have been accomplished in the period before the prophets.[14]

The Expansions of the Commandment to Honour Parents, Ex. 20.12

The expansion of Ex. 20.12 consists of a concluding clause
which provides a special kind of reason for the commandment.
The basic idea is, of course, not that obedience to parents leads
automatically to the attainment of a long life, but that those
who show respect to and care for their parents are rewarded
by Yahweh with length of life on the plot of land which he has
bestowed upon them. Changed into the style of v. 7: 'For
Yahweh gives a long life to him who honours his father and his
mother.' While the turn of phrase 'on the plot of ground which
Yahweh your God gives you' is held to be wholly Deuteronomist in style,[15] the expression 'that thy days may be long', i.e.
that a long life may be attained, has a history of its own. It is
very frequent in the Deuteronomist literature (with the Hiphil
variously used to express interior and exterior causality:
Deut. 4.26, 40; 5.30; 6.2; 11.9; 17.20; 22.7; 25.15 and 30.18,
to mention only the passages in Deuteronomy itself). But
passages such as Isa. 53.10, from the song of the Suffering Servant
of Yahweh, owe nothing beyond this to the Deuteronomists,
but are indebted far more to the royal psalms, the language
and thought-sequence of which is echoed throughout the entire

[12] See pp. 112ff. below on the basic causes of the alteration of negative formulations to positive ones.
[13] The sabbath as taboo day: Amos 8.5; Jer. 17.19ff. The sabbath as festival
day: Hos. 2.11; Isa. 1.13; II Kings 4.23; 11.5-7.
[14] Cf. previous note, the sabbath as a festival day. In Lev. 19.3 the positive
formulation is also presupposed.
[15] Deut. 4.40; 7.13; 11.9, 21; 12.1; 25.15; 26.2, 10, 15; 28.11; 30. 20.

song (Isa. 52.13-53.12).[16] In this connection Ps. 91.16 calls for special notice: 'I swore to give him length of life (*'ōrek yāmīm*), and I will show him my salvation.' These are the concluding words of a royal psalm liturgy. Cf. also Ps. 23.6, the concluding words of a 'psalm of confidence', which may very well count as a royal psalm, and finally Ps. 21.4, which says of the king: 'Thou gavest him the life that he asked of thee, *a long life* for ever and ever.' In this connection it may be mentioned that the desire to have long life bestowed on one is a constantly recurring theme in Phoenician royal inscriptions.[17]

Setting aside the varied origins of the particular elements in the expansions of the command to honour parents, it can be stated with some degree of certainty that the expansion as such presupposes the transformation from the negative to the positive form. But the 'promise' which is connected with the latter, may very well have acquired part of its content from the context in which the decalogue was originally found. In this connection it should be noticed that Ps. 15, the nearest parallel to the decalogue among the psalms, concludes its list of prohibitions with the declaration, 'He who does these things shall never be moved', Ps. 15.5.

The Expansions of 'You shall not Covet', Ex. 20.17

We have here a verbal repetition of the negation and verb followed by a list of objects all of which—like the object in

---

[16] Cf. especially Ivan Engnell, 'The Ebed Yahweh Songs and the Suffering Messiah in "Deutero-Isaiah" ', *BJRL* 31, 1948, pp. 54-93. Also 'Herrens Tjänare' (The Servant of the Lord), *Svenskt Bibliskt Uppslagsverk.* 1, 2nd ed. 1962, pp. 940-943.

[17] The inscription of Yeḥimilk King of Byblos (tenth century BC), 11.3-5ff.: 'May Ba'al Shamen and the Lord of Byblos and the Assembly of the Holy Gods of Byblos prolong the days and years of Yeḥimilk in Byblos, for (he is) a righteous king and upright king in the eyes of the holy gods of Byblos.' The inscription of Eliba'al of Byblos (about the end of the tenth century BC), 11.2-3: 'May the Ba'alat of Byblos prolong Eliba'al's days and years over Byblos.' See also the inscription of Šipit-Ba'al of Byblos about 900 BC, and that of *Yeḥawmilk* of Byblos from the 5th century, 1.9, likewise adducing the righteousness of the king as a motive. Text in Donner/Röllig, *Kanaanäische und aramäische Inschriften I*, 1962, pp. 1-2, Translation and Commentary by the same, *Kanaanäische und aramäische Inschriften II*, 1964, pp. 6-15. [The first and third of these inscriptions also appear in *ANET*, pp. 499 and 502. Tr.]

v. 17a—are qualified by the phrase 'thy neighbour' in the genitive. The one question which might be raised at this point is whether the expansion may be regarded as a commentary on the prohibition of covetousness proper, and, to put it another way, as defining what is included under the term 'thy neighbour's house'. Or, alternatively the object of expanding the phrase may be that the expression 'thy neighbour's house' is understood in a wholly literal sense as referring to the actual building in which 'thy neighbour' lives, so that v. 17b would represent an expansion of the prohibition of covetousness. Probably the expansion should be regarded as having been, from the outset, a definition of what is included in the idea of 'house' over and above the actual material of which it is constructed, and, so far as its content goes, this definition is early (see our observations above with regard to the eighth commandment and its original formulation).[18] But that in the period of the Deuteronomists it is understood as a new commandment is shown by the interchange of the elements 'house' and 'wife' which these humanist theologians have made, and which, moreover, is emphasised by the fact that the second occurrence of the prohibition of covetousness is varied by the use of *hit'awweh*, 'to lust after'.

3. THE SECONDARY ABBREVIATIONS OF THE DECALOGUE

Three of the ten commandments of the decalogue have clearly been given in an abbreviated form, namely the prohibitions of adultery, killing and theft.

The Abbreviation to 'You shall not commit Adultery', Ex. 20.14

The prohibition of adultery, in the reconstruction of which we have taken Lev. 20.10 as our model (incidentally it has been repeated twice here through a scribal error), has a quite precise content: it forbids a man to intrude into the marriage of an-

---

[18] Cf. p. 91. above and A. Alt, 'Das Verbot des Diebstahls im Dekalog', *Kleine Schriften* I, 1953, pp. 339f.

other by seducing his wife. Now the question is 'What can have been the motive for excising the object, i.e. for having cut something out of this clear and concise prohibition?' It can hardly have been done, it seems, for juridical reasons. We know from casuistic law that the jurist always strives to give the most unequivocal formulation possible to his laws even when he has to multiply words in order to do so. Now in what has previously been said we have already touched several times on the collections of apodictic commandments which are essentially concerned with offences in the sexual sphere. These appear in their final formulation in the Code of Holiness (Lev. 17-26), the ultimate redaction of which presumably belongs to the late pre-exilic period.[1] Two elements which have already engaged our attention are the original decalogue form of the rules of behaviour for members of the extended family, the basic element in Lev. 18.7-18, and also the *mōt yūmāt* laws of Lev. 20, a chapter which, as we have seen, begins with laws forbidding child sacrifice (v. 2), and goes on to prohibit the use of various forms of (Gentile) soothsaying techniques (v. 6); then in v. 10 we encounter the law against adultery, which we have used in reconstructing the sixth commandment of the decalogue. We have drawn particular attention to these three passages in the law because they all have a contribution to make in explaining why we have the sixth commandment of the decalogue only in

---

[1] On the Holiness Code cf. especially *Untersuchungen zum Heiligkeitsgesetz*, published postumously in 1962 after the untimely death of its author, Christian Feucht. He regarded 'H 1' (Lev. 18-23A) as pre-Deuteronomist, and 'H 2' (Lev. 25-26) as stemming from the period after Josiah's reform but before the exile. Lev. 17; 23B and 24A are not considered by Feucht to have belonged to the original Holiness Code (*op. cit.* pp. 166-180). A further significant work must here be mentioned, that of Henning Graf Reventlow, *Das Heiligkeitsgesetz*, 1961. The basis of the form-critical approach which Reventlow adopts is the conception of the Holiness Code as a liturgical document, the original 'setting in life' of which was the Israelite covenant festival. He rejects the idea that the Holiness Code would have been composed during the exile or at the period of the exile, and strongly emphasizes that extremely early material is to be found in it. For the rest, his praiseworthy efforts to achieve a synthetic view of the Holiness Code have nevertheless contributed to stamp his work with a slight neglect of analytic approach. In his *Israel* III-IV, 1940, p. 341, Johannes Pedersen has appositely summed up the character of the Holiness Code in the following terms: 'The remarkable collection of statutes, in which purely abstract commands are found side by side with early Israelite rules.'

an abbreviated form. After the statement of the punishment for adultery in Lev. 20.10, *mōt yūmāt*, '*he* shall surely die' the phrase *hanno'ēp w^ehanno'āpet*, 'the adulterer and the adulteress alike' is added. In other words both the man and also the wife of the other man are liable to the penalty. The question may reasonably be asked whether the abbreviation did not have a juridical interest behind it, namely that the sixth commandment of the decalogue applies to married women too. Still it must be admitted that the formulation of the verb, which is in the second person singular masculine, tells against this. Nevertheless the law forbidding recourse to the spirits of the dead and practising the invocation of spirits (v. 6) does contain an addition which can throw a clearer light upon the motives which led to the abbreviation of the sixth commandment of the decalogue. In this passage one who has recourse to the spirits of the dead is said to 'play the harlot after' them, *liznōt 'aḥᵃrēhem*. In other words the adoption of Gentile practices of soothsaying is here regarded as religious infidelity. And the solemnity of tone with which the reason for forbidding child sacrifice is expressed in v. 3b corresponds perfectly to this: 'He has given one of his children to *molk*, defiling my sanctuary and profaning my holy name.' We find a similar line of thought, according to which religious apostasy is described as marital infidelity to Yahweh on the part of the people, especially in the three prophets Hosea, Jeremiah and Ezekiel. From the end of the eighth century onwards this became a comprehensible manner of speaking for the Israelites and Judahites, and hence the abbreviated formulation of the sixth commandment came in this way to be directed not only against every form of sexual offence (including sodomy and homosexuality) but also against religious apostasy. The ultimate proof of this is that an expression has been employed which is derived from the actual technical term itself, namely 'adultery', *nā'ap* (intensive form *ni'ēp*). As used by Hosea (2.4; 3.1; 4.2, 13, 14; 7.4) this still has the literal meaning 'breach of marriage', but is at the same time used figuratively, especially in 2.4 and 3.1, perhaps also in 7.4. In Jeremiah it is used in a series of passages in the applied sense of religious apostasy (Jer. 3.8, 9; 5.7; 9.1), while Ezekiel in his well-known allegories in chs. 16 and 23 uses the term partly like Hosea in a consciously figurative sense (Ezek. 16.32 in the feminine), partly as Jeremiah uses it in an applied sense (Ezek. 23.37). By this expression the sixth commandment advanced a long way in the direction in which the decalogue in general was tending by its very nature, that is, to embrace within its ten short commandments as much as possible of the content of apodictic law.

The Abbreviation to 'You shall not Kill', Ex. 20.13

From the discussions among both laymen and specialists concerning the content of the law against killing, it is abundantly clear that this cannot be said to be unambiguous. One fact which will be clear from the outset to all whose knowledge of the Old Testament is more than superficial is that it is no part of the purpose of this commandment to rule out the death penalty or the waging of war. Both were present in Israel as far back as we can trace her history or, if we proceed in the opposite direction, up to the time when the Jews were deprived of the right of imposing or exacting the death penalty under the alien rule of Rome. From the numerous investigations which have been undertaken into the use of the term employed in the seventh commandment of the decalogue, namely *rāṣaḥ*,[2] it has been established that this word may be used both of deliberate and of accidental killing, and furthermore, virtually all its occurrences are connected with the institution of asylum. The relevant passages, apart from the decalogue and those dependent upon it (Hos. 4.2; Jer. 7.9), are to be found in Num. 35; Deut. 4.42; 19.3-6; 22.26; Josh. 20-21. The exceptions are I Kings 21.19, where Elijah is given the task of accusing Ahab of murder, *rāṣaḥtā*, 'thou hast murdered' (after the sham trial of Naboth), and Job 24.14, where the participle *rōṣēaḥ* is used of

---

[2] Cf. J. J. Stamm, 'Sprachliche Erwägungen zum Gebot "Du sollst nicht töten" ', *TZ* 1, 1945, pp. 81-90, and further in *TR*, NF 27, 1962, pp. 296-298. On the connection with the institution of asylum and blood-vengeance see Henning Graf Reventlow, *Gebot und Predigt im Dekalog*, 1962, pp. 71-77.

the murderer who slays the poor without pity.[3] The institution
of asylum belongs to the period of settlement in the land. In
earlier times the altar of any holy place may perhaps have
served as an asylum as well, to which one accused of murder
could flee for refuge to escape those bent on exacting blood
vengeance. In the course of time certain of the larger sanctuaries proved particularly suitable as places of asylum, and in the
Deuteronomist reform, which had the effect of abolishing the
sacral character of the local shrines, these holy places were still
maintained as asylum *towns*, three on either side of the Jordan
(cf. Deut. 4.43 and 19.3; Josh. 20.7ff.). If our reconstruction
of the seventh commandment, with its prohibition of pouring
out the blood of one's neighbour, is right, this would of course
have applied to private killing, but would have been quite
irrelevant to the imposition or execution of the death penalty,
to killing in war or to blood vengeance, which is simply war at
its most primitive. And if this is correct, then those who *altered*
the seventh commandment presumably had in mind the institution of blood-vengeance. This seems to have been custom,
usage and law throughout long periods in the history of Israel,
and only to have been weakened in connection with the general
weakening of tribal and family ties, a general weakening which
does in fact usually affect a people when it remains for whole
generations settled on the land, and especially when it comes
into contact with urban culture. The clearest example of such
a weakening of the institution of blood-vengeance is found in
II Kings 14.5f., where King Amaziah is said to have had killed
those of his people who had co-operated in the murder of his
father, but on the other hand omitted to kill the children of the
murderers. The explicit reference to the Mosaic book of the law
in v. 6 is, of course, Deuteronomist, and is connected with
Deut. 24.16: 'The fathers shall not be put to death for the
children, nor shall the children be put to death for the fathers.
Every man shall be put to death for his own sin.' The alteration
of the seventh commandment, therefore, does not signify any

---

[3] We have omitted altogether those passages in which *raṣaḥ* is used in the intensive mood.

generalizing of the prohibition of private killing, but is rather an element in the struggle against the institution of blood-vengeance, and is in perfect agreement with a growing individualism and, together with this, a weakening of the sense of historical connections.[4]

The Abbreviation to 'You shall not Steal', Ex. 20.15

In discussing the original content of this commandment considerations have already engaged our attention which affect the relationship between this prohibition and that of covetousness. Against the theory, formerly so much favoured, that the final commandment of the decalogue is an expression of the ethics of interior disposition, we have noticed the more recent theory as to the meaning of the verb 'covet', *ḥāmad*. In reality it designates the act of appropriating something, so that the difference between the eighth and the tenth commandment consists primarily in a difference of objects. In the eighth commandment it is the free Israelite man, in the tenth the 'house' of the Israelite man, i.e. women, slaves both male and female, cattle and all possessions belonging to him. The abbreviation of the formulation of the eighth commandment, therefore, must be connected with an altered understanding of what the verb *ḥāmad* really imports, this accompanied by a psychologizing tendency which culminates in Deut. 5.21, where *ḥāmad* is made equivalent to *hit'awwe*.

Although we can make no general assertion as to when the commandments of the decalogue underwent their expansions we have more chance of arriving at a conclusion on this point in the case of the abbreviations. For in at least four passages in the Old Testament we find allusions to the decalogue which appear to presuppose the short formulations of the sixth, seventh and eighth commandments. The passages are: Hos. 4.2; Jer.

---

[4] I once regarded it as possible that the abbreviation of the seventh commandment could be viewed as connected with the eschatologically orientated preaching of paradise and the kingdom of peace as encountered in the prophets of the eighth and seventh centuries BC. Now, however, influenced by the enlightening expositions of Reventlow (see above n. 2), I have abandoned my earlier position.

7.9; Lev. 19.11; Job 24.14-15. It may prove difficult to assign a date to the two last, and for this reason we shall confine ourselves to statements concerning one of the passages, namely Lev. 19.11. That this is secondary in relation to the decalogue appears from three facts: first, the verbs are in the second person plural, secondly, the prohibition of killing and of adultery are omitted, and thirdly, the generalizing tendency exemplified in certain of the abbreviations is carried further. Thus the prohibition of bearing false witness may be translated as follows: 'Thou shalt not lie and thou shalt not deceive thy neighbour.' Jeremiah, who shows himself at many points to be influenced by the line of thought expressed in Hosea, can also show dependence in his citations of the decalogue on the Hosean tradition. The passage in Hosea, therefore, provides our principal witness for the *terminus ante quem* of the abbreviations in the decalogue. At the beginning of his fourth chapter the prophet complains that there is no faithfulness or kindness, and no knowledge of God in the land.[5] To illustrate this he enumerates in the verses immediately following the sins of perjury, killing, stealing, adultery, violence and bloodshed. The connection of 'killing' (the term employed is *rāṣaḥ*) and bloodshed is interesting in itself because it confirms the correctness of the thesis stated above that the seventh commandment of the decalogue in the form in which we have it today is directed particularly against blood-vengeance and not merely against killing in general. As to the sequence of Hosea's enumeration, it is clear that the order of the clauses of the decalogue cannot be recon-

---

[5] On the basis of Hos. 4.4ff. Joachim Begrich (in *Die priesterliche Tora*, 1936, p. 86) lays great emphasis upon the fact that *dā'at 'elōhim* is the specialized knowledge of the priests, whereas *tōrā* is priestly instruction of the laity. We have shown above that we are opposed to his rigid division between the cultic and ritualistic preaching of the priests, and the moral preaching of the prophets. Moreover the passage in Hos. 4.2, in which transgressions of the decalogue are adduced as an illustration of the lack of *dā'at*, demonstrates the inapplicability of such a precise division. Cf. also the close parallelism in Hos. 6 between 'loyal devotion', *ḥesed*, and *dā'at 'elōhim*, 'knowledge of God'. The fact that the quotation from the decalogue is introduced immediately after the lament over the lack of *dā'at could* be adduced to support the argument that the handing down of the decalogue was a sacred responsibility of the priests. See below pp. 128ff., our treatment of the question of whether the decalogue is to be understood as an address by Yahweh.

structed from this. It begins with a paraphrasing description of the third and ninth commandment, and then goes on immediately to mention the three commandments of the decalogue now given in a short formulation together. In this connection it may be remarked that in Jeremiah (7.9) the order of the commandments is: theft, murder, adultery, false swearing, serving strange gods (that is, the eighth, seventh, sixth, third and first commandments).

4. THE CHANGING OF NEGATIVE FORMULATIONS INTO POSITIVE ONES

Two commandments of the decalogue in the form in which we have them today are formulated positively; the sabbath commandment and the commandment to honour parents.

The Sabbath Commandment, Ex. 20.8

We have already said something above of the theory that the character of the sabbath, originally a taboo day, was later altered in the sense that it became a festival day at the same time.[1] We have also said that the alteration of the prohibition of doing work on the sabbath into a commandment to observe the sabbath and keep it holy must be viewed in the light of this theory. In this connection we propose only to draw attention to a single detail in connection with the transformation of the sabbath commandment. A brief survey of the collections of laws, some of them ancient, with which we have been concerned in our investigation, namely the Book of the Covenant, the Holiness Code and Deuteronomy, will make it immediately apparent that there is one particular type of law which we have largely neglected hitherto. This is the type of the cultic laws of the Old Testament, that is, the prescriptions for sacrifices and festivals, sacral offerings and rituals. It is a formal characteristic of these cultic laws that they are for the most part formulated positively; they are commandments, not prohibitions. This applies to the statute which we find among the laws

[1] See above, pp. 102f.

framing the Book of the Covenant, Ex. 20.24 and 23.10ff.: 'An altar of earth you shall make for me, and sacrifice on it your burnt offerings and your peace offerings, your sheep and your oxen' (20.24a), and 'three times in the year you shall keep a feast to me. You shall keep the feast of unleavened bread as I commanded you. You shall eat unleavened bread for seven days at the appointed time in the month of Abib, for in it you came out of Egypt', etc. (23.14ff.). Admittedly a series of subordinate prescriptions are formulated in the negative as prohibitions, Ex. 20.25f. and 23.15c, 18a and b, 19b, but the chief commandments are in the affirmative. The passage in Ex. 34 which is parallel to Ex. 23 exhibits the same traits. Here too the sabbath commandment is formulated in the affirmative (34.21): 'Six days you shall work but on the seventh day you shall keep the sabbath. Even during (the time) of ploughing and harvesting you shall keep the sabbath.' Here the verb *šābat* is used simply as a denominative of *šabbāt*, that is without the explicit emphasis on the meaning 'rest' or 'cease from something' which it has in Gen. 2.2 (where it occurs with preposition + object, *mikkol-meʾlaʾktō*, 'from all his work'). It is possible that in its present position in a series of laws concerning the three principal festivals of the year the sabbath law in Ex. 34 occurs as an alien element. The commandment in 23.12 appears more in place, for here it stands in the closest parallelism with the commandment concerning the year of release, 23.10-11. These two commandments, together with the exhortation in v. 13, represent a transition from the Book of the Covenant and its 'model for the judge' to the cultic laws in vv. 14ff., which constitute a distinct section. The motives behind these two laws of the sabbath and the year of release are social and charitable considerations. The poor must receive nourishment and domestic beasts must be able to rest. These motives clearly presuppose the settled life of Canaanite culture, with its vineyards and olive groves, oxen and asses. When one recalls the part played by the seven-year period in the introduction to the Book of the Covenant proper, that is, in the laws concerning slaves, Ex. 21.2ff., one realizes that this, together with the passage just considered, makes the Book of the Covenant a well-rounded whole, and Alt's well-known hypothesis to the effect that the Deuteronomist statement in Deut. 31.9-13 rests upon ancient tradition appears not in the least arbitrary.[2] For in this law of Deut. 31.9ff. the people of Israel are commanded to hold at the festival of Tabernacles *every seven years* a special ceremonial reading of the law, 'that they may hear and learn to fear Yahweh and observe all the words of the law', 31.12.

In these prescriptions, in which the number seven plays an essential part, we encounter a mixture of negative and affirmative: the Hebrew slave who has been bought shall work for six years, but in the seventh year he shall go free; a man shall sow his land and gather his harvest during six years, but in the seventh year he shall let it lie fallow; a man shall do his work for six days, but on the seventh day he shall keep the sabbath. Yet underlying the affirmative formulation in these instances is something which might equally well be formulated negatively: In the seventh year the Hebrew man shall *no longer* be a slave; in the seventh year the land shall *not* be sown; on the seventh day work shall *not* be done. What we encounter here is a connection which is both formal and material between laws which belong to different literary categories, and this serves to indicate that from the earliest history of Israel onwards the sabbath law exercised an especially powerful influence on the Hebrew mind. The privileged position which the sabbath law occupies in the decalogue fully accords with this, and the fact that the commandment is formulated in the affirmative in the decalogue is wholly consistent with our finding with regard to the laws encountered in the Book of the Covenant. Together with the laws of the year of release the sabbath commandment has a certain affinity with the cultic laws,[3] yet appears from the outset unaffected by any element pertaining to the cult or sanctuary, contrasting in this respect with the laws concerning sacrifices, festivals and rituals.

[2] A. Alt, 'Origins . . .', pp. 126-32; cf. also von Rad, 'The form-critical Problem . . .', pp. 34f.
[3] On the year of release cf. the definition in Deut. 31.9ff.

The Commandment to Honour Parents, Ex. 20.12

In its existing formulation this commandment is far from unambiguous. Because of this it has inevitably become the subject of the most varied interpretations. One possibility is to regard it as addressed to the young man who is unwilling to submit to the authority of the head of the family, a conception which is in conformity with the law in Deut. 21.18-21, prescribing that a recalcitrant and dissolute son is to be stoned. The commandment can also be understood as meaning that a man must care for his aged parents and not neglect them when they need support, and this interpretation is probably the most natural, partly because the rest of the commandments of the decalogue are not 'instruction for children' in the literal sense, partly because a special kind of promise is attached to this commandment, namely a promise of a long and happy life for the free Israelite citizen or peasant. Of the three commandments in apodictic law which appear as counterparts to our affirmatively formulated commandment two (the prohibition of cursing parents and that of despising them, Ex. 21.17 or Deut. 27.16) are most naturally explained in terms of the latter interpretation, while the other, the prohibition of striking one's parents, Ex. 21.15, is more in harmony with the former one. Perhaps, however, the fact that this commandment can now be given a broader interpretation than if it were in the form of a prohibition can be regarded as a not altogether accidental consequence of the change from prohibition to positive commandment.

The desire to broaden the application of this commandment as far as possible, however, is hardly significant enough in itself to explain the reformulation. For the question is whether in this case, as in that of the sabbath, there could have been analogies (as the cultic commandments provide analogies for the sabbath) which would explain why an affirmative formulation has been preferred in this case. Here we come back to Gerstenberger's theory of an original connection between the Old Testament 'prohibitives' and the exhortations and warnings of the Wisdom literature.[4] In this connection there is a special reason for drawing attention to the collection of maxims in Prov. 1-9. A single quotation may be sufficient for our purpose:

> Hear, O sons, a father's instruction,
> and be attentive, that you may gain insight;
> for I give you good precepts;
> do not forsake my teaching.
> When I was a son with my father,
> tender, the only one in the sight of my mother,
> he taught me and said to me,
> 'Let your heart hold fast my words;
> keep my commandments and live;
> do not forget, and do not turn
> away from the words of my mouth.'
>
> (Prov. 4.1-5)

In this passage the affirmative form is absolutely predominant, the negative appearing only in complementary warnings. The Wisdom teacher among his pupils is in the relationship of a father to his children.[5] He must show them the right way, the way that leads to life.[6]

We have spoken of the allegedly *original* connection between the Wisdom literature and apodictic law in the Old Testament. It is no part of our belief, however, that the affirmative form of this commandment to pay respect to parents stems specifically from this. Rather this affirmative form may be explained as a transformation that has taken place under the influence of the Wis-

---

[4] Gerstenberger, *Wesen und Herkunft* . . . , 1961, pp. 59-117.

[5] In the course of an attempt to show that 'tribal morality' was the *fons et origo* of law-giving and of the Wisdom literature, Gerstenberger introduces an element which is wholly justified, and which lends emphasis to the fact that the designation 'father' was applied to the teacher of Wisdom, the priest (Judg. 17.10) and also to the prophet (II Kings 2.12). Cf. especially *op. cit.* pp. 95ff.

[6] However, we encounter the same theme again in what is clearly a *cultic* context in Ezek. 18.5ff., where the declaration of assent 'Let him live' is found immediately following upon the assertion 'he is righteous'. See above, pp. 23ff. With regard to the concluding exhortation of the Deuteronomists in Deut. 30.15ff., in which the Israelites are faced with a choice between life and death, happiness and misfortune, it would be difficult to decide whether this owes more to the Wisdom literature or to the sacral tradition.

dom literature, and the effect of this transformation upon the commandment to pay heed to parents is entirely typical. It is true of Old Testament literature in general that an approximation can be established between the Wisdom literature and the rest of the literary categories. For instance it is clear in the case of the psalms, and Ps. 19 can be taken here as a perfect example. In this psalm ancient mythical conceptions of Yahweh as the sun whose gaze no mortal creature can escape are combined with praise of Yahweh's law, which is perfect, reliable, just, pure, true, more precious than gold and sweeter than honey. These very skilful variations of eulogies are set side by side with no less skilful designations of Yahweh's law. We find expressions such as '*ēdūt Yahweh*, 'Yahweh's testimony', *piqqūdē Yahweh*, 'Yahweh's precepts', *miṣwat Yahweh*, 'Yahweh's command', *yir'at Yahweh*, 'fear of Yahweh', and *mišpᵉṭē Yahweh*, 'Yahweh's ordinances', all synonymous, and without any advertence to the original 'setting in life' of the various expressions employed. This suggests not only that this psalm cannot be regarded as particularly early, but also that the composer of the psalm has been influenced by the Wisdom literature. In this connection one further point must be noticed. In this Ps. 19 it is said that the law and the observance of the law bring rich and assured blessings to those who observe it. It brings life to men, makes fools wise, fills the heart with joy, enlightens the eyes. Finally in v. 12 we are told that keeping Yahweh's commandments brings a great reward.

Manifestly here the influence of the sages has led to an altered concept of what the function of law is. Law still continues to have its earlier function of marking out the bounds laid down by the terms of the covenant, and of defining the sphere within which the life of the Israelites could take its normal course: 'By them is thy servant warned' (v. 11). But the law becomes at the same time a positive stimulus to undertake certain courses of action. The future reward for its observance beckons the Israelite on. It takes the form of blessings which are allotted to him who is 'devoted to the law'.[7] Now the significance of the

---

[7] The original function of the law was to define the limits of the covenant, and

positive formulation 'Honour your father and your mother', together with the addition 'that your days may be long in the land which Yahweh your God gives you' is that the decalogue too has been made to give expression to this new function of the law.

The background of this in terms of actual history can hardly be determined with any exactitude. Yet we cannot be far wrong in our assumptions if we take it that the reason why the fifth commandment of the decalogue has been so powerfully emphasized by being formulated in the affirmative may be the loosening of family ties entailed by an increasingly urban culture. The motif of 'the bad sons' is one of which we are made powerfully aware in the prophetic preaching of the eighth and seventh centuries in the northern (Hos. 11.1ff.) and southern kingdoms (Isa. 1.2f.; Micah 7.5f.) alike, and is often used to characterize the circumstances of a community in process of dissolution and of religious apostasy. But it can hardly be correct to assume that such a process would have been confined exclusively to the eighth and seventh centuries. It is surely nearer the truth to say that at all periods the culture developed in larger urban centres made it especially easy for family ties to be loosened and for respect towards the older generation to be diminished.

5. SUMMARY

As our working hypothesis we have taken the idea that the present form of the decalogue is in part due to the fact that in the course of time it has been subjected to additions, abbreviations and modifications. These alterations were made in the course of what was presumably a long history of tradition. In

hence it was basically connected with the cursing of the law-breaker, and not with the blessing of the devout observer of the law. On this see especially M. Noth, ' "For All who Rely on Works of the Law are under a Curse" ', ET in *The Laws in the Pentateuch and Other Studies*, 1966, pp. 118-131. See also 'The Laws in the Pentateuch', *op. cit.*, pp. 1-107, especially chapter 4, ' "The Law" as an Absolute Entity during the Late Period', pp. 85-103, particularly pp. 100ff. Also von Rad, *Old Testament Theology*, I, pp. 90-92 and 198-203.

determining their *extent* our chosen method has been that of
the form-critical approach, and by means of this we have
attempted to reconstruct the original form of the decalogue.
Our aim has been, then, to account in detail for each of the
alterations to which, as we see it, the decalogue has been subjected. The task that now lies before us consists in providing a
survey of the tradition-history of the decalogue, while drawing
together all our individual conclusions, so that as a result of our
researches we can present a history which is, as far as possible,
consistent within itself. We emphasized above the hypothetical
character of our reconstruction. A similar emphasis must, of
course, be applied here. For even when the best methods have
been employed for such a task as that which lies before us, still
the difficulty always remains that the source material available
to throw light upon the culture of the Israelite people in pre-
exilic times is in fact fragmentary.[1]

We propose to commence, therefore, by establishing an
upper and lower time-limit. The form in which we have the
decalogue today (in Ex. 20) goes back to some point between
622 and 560 BC. Moreover certain elements are to be found in
the decalogue, both in its original form and with its secondary
additions, which point back quite clearly to the period at which
the religion of Yahweh became the religion of Israel.

The historical sources available to throw light upon the
earliest history of Israel provide only sparse information. So far
as the period of the entry of the Israelite tribes into Canaan is
concerned we cannot recapture enough of the actual facts in
their historical detail to give an account of the sequence of
events in this part of Israel's history which has a sound basis in
the principles of scientific historical criticism. It is not until the
beginning of the period of the kings that history in this sense
becomes possible. When we reach this period, however, we can
ask ourselves the question 'What was the characteristic stamp
of the religion of Israel at this time in relation to neighbouring
cultures?', and from considerations bearing upon this question

---

[1] A fact recognized in theory by the majority of scholars, but not always borne
in mind in the course of their discussions!

we can permit ourselves to draw certain more general conclusions.

The first four commandments of the decalogue all refer back to the time before the entry into the land. The Yahweh whom they reflect is Yahweh the jealous, who will not tolerate any recourse to another god on the part of those who elect to honour him. This jealousy of his also applies to the images which men might be tempted to set up in order to express in symbolic form what God means to them. Quite regardless of the offences committed against this commandment in the course of Israel's history (Judg. 17f.; I Kings 12 etc.; II Kings 18.4), the prohibition of images in its original form reveals an attitude of mind which is typical of nomad culture. The stipulation that the holiness of the name 'Yahweh' must be preserved from misuse for magical purposes is entirely in harmony with this, and in sharp contrast to the intermingling of religion and magic in the great civilizations nearby. Finally let us recall our surmise that in the period before the religion of Yahweh became attached to the tribal confederation of Israel its devotees were chiefly to be found among the Kenites. These, as their very name implies, were especially engaged in the craft of metal work and forging. If this surmise is correct, then, it follows that the prohibition of work upon the sabbath day also is particularly appropriate to the nomadic stage. Thus an element is brought to light in what might be called the true Mosaic tradition—that strand in the later Israelite culture which did not let itself be seduced by the numerous manifestations of the Canaanite way of life in the land—which dominates all the rest together: the idea of Yahweh as a jealous God.[2] In the decalogue the first four commandments are permeated by this thought. In v. 5b Yahweh is explicitly described as *'ēl qannā'*, 'a jealous God', and while from a form-critical point of

[2] Probably no one has expressed this so appositely as F. F. Hvidberg in his account of the Mosaic religion as presented in his work 'Tro og Moral. Den israelitiske Religions Historie' (Faith and Morals. The History of the Israelite Religion), *Haandbog i Kristendomskundskab* II, ed, A. Bentzen, 1943, pp. 204-375, especially pp. 243-248. It is a pleasure to acknowledge with gratitude how much I owe to his scholarship and his direction, not least in its bearing upon this point of fundamental importance.

view this is secondary, at any rate in the place in which it now
stands, nevertheless it is an addition that conforms to the facts
and expresses what is most of all the characteristic stamp of
Israelite religion.

Let us now pass on from the first four commandments of the
decalogue and examine the last six commandments in closer
detail in the form in which we have attempted to reconstruct
them. Here it is not so easy to decide whether it is the voice of
nomadic culture that we hear or that of the land after the settlement. Kidnapping, adultery, false accusations, appropriation
of another man's possessions, murder, disrespect to parents—
the condemnation of these offences is no less firmly rooted in
the nomadic way of life than in the order prevailing in a
peasant society. The most obvious piece of evidence on which
to base a hypothesis with regard to the underlying social structure is the object which is forbidden to be coveted, namely 'your
neighbour's house'. Now according to the way in which the
content of Ex. 20.17b has been interpreted this is to be understood as envisaging the 'family'. Against this it can be said that
the ox and ass in v. 17b in this passage clearly set us in the
context of the settled way of life in the land.

However *in its present form* the decalogue contains other formulations, which clearly emphasize that the institutions of the
settled way of life have also left a clear impress upon the decalogue. We are thinking here primarily of the alteration of the
law against honouring any other god besides Yahweh. In this
the expression 'before my countenance' clearly belongs to the
language of these institutions. It does not contradict the prohibition of images, for the presence of God does not need to be
represented by a symbolic image of him. But the expression
presupposes the existence of one or several shrines, to which
one can go in order to 'look upon Yahweh's countenance'.[3] It

---

[3] For later Jewish tradition this expression became too strong: therefore the verbal forms are vocalized as Niphals, and so interpreted in the sense of 'appearing
before'; cf. Pss. 42.3; 84.8; Ex. 23.15; 34.23. In addition to the verb $r\bar{a}'\bar{a}$, 'to see',
$h\bar{a}z\bar{a}$, 'to behold' (Ps. 17.15) and $biqqe\check{s}$, 'to seek' (Pss. 24.6 and 27.8) are also
used. To behold Yahweh's countenance is to experience his manifestation or his
apparition. This can be in an oracle, a sacral ordeal, in the issue of victory or
defeat, in the course of a ritual drama, etc.

is only natural that in this connection the basic commandment not to honour other gods should be attached to the sanctuary traditions. It is therefore a more reasonable conclusion, one more in conformity with the facts, if not actually a necessary one that at some point the tradition of the decalogue must have been handed down as a 'shrine' tradition, i.e. in priestly circles in particular.

We have seen that the transformation of the sabbath commandment in the decalogue has its forerunners in the prescriptions of the Book of the Covenant. In the Book of the Covenant the sabbath day already appears as not merely a day of rest but a festival day too. Admittedly the sabbath law as it appears in the Book of the Covenant stands in an isolated position immediately following upon the conclusion of the Book of the Covenant proper, the 'model for a judge', and immediately preceding the secondary framework of cultic laws. Our observations on the role of the number seven both in the Book of the Covenant itself and in the law concerning the sabbath and the year of release led us, however, to conclude that the most probable assumption was that the laws in Ex. 23.10-12 (13) represent a genuinely integral element of the Book of the Covenant. There is no evidence to support the view that the Book of the Covenant presupposes the social structure of the period of the monarchy at any point. It should rather be regarded as an expression of the law-making of the period of Judges. In the well-known reference in II Kings 4.23 we possess quite unambiguous evidence for the observance of the sabbath in the positive sense which dates from the ninth century BC. The alteration of the sabbath commandment itself from a prohibition to a commandment, therefore, can be explained very well against the background of the period of Judges and the religious circumstances of the period of the first kings. By contrast the reason given for the sabbath commandment brings us down to somewhat later times. Here we encounter a conception of the world which is wholly in conformity with the cultic traditions of the settled way of life, and which has no contact whatever with the Bedouin mentality.

The period extending from the reign of Solomon to the downfall of the dynasty of Omri in the middle of the ninth century BC is characterized by an ever-strengthening challenge to the early Israelite traditions of nomadic and peasant culture. As early as the time of David Israel had come to engage herself in earnest in the sphere of international politics, and the ensuing period is strongly marked by the economic and social consequences of this fact. A new social structure is created, working downwards from above, by the organization of administrative classes which cut across the old tribal boundaries. Royal household and central sanctuary represent further factors leading to an altered outlook and way of life. The cultural horizon is radically changed and broadened, while at the same time traditional ideas undergo a crisis. G. von Rad has characterized this epoch as a 'free-thinking era'.[4] He regards it as the best preparation for the emergence of a conception of mankind and of history on a universal scale, and this in turn provides the basic structure underlying the earlier source material of the Tetrateuch. Here the old local traditions are detached from their ties to specific shrines, and fitted into an overall view of history. The basic nucleus in this process is constituted by the central themes of salvation history as set forth in the 'historical credo' of Israel: the liberation from Egypt and the entry into Canaan. The stories of the patriarchs and the tradition of the wilderness wandering are firmly attached to salvation history, and the overall view of history is rounded off by the addition of the primaeval history of mankind from the Creation to the building of the Tower of Babel, and including the Flood. Here Israel appears as the elect people chosen from the lost world of the Gentiles, chosen to bring God's blessing to all peoples. This 'free-thinking era' also provides the necessary conditions for the blossoming of the earlier Wisdom literature, characterized by a lively interest in all earthly things.

In all this a desire for synthesis can be discerned which would fit in well with the systematic drawing up of the basic rules of

[4] On this cf. especially *Genesis* ET(OTL) 1961, pp. 13-30; *Old Testament Theology* I, pp. 48-56. On the earlier Wisdom literature see *ibid.*, pp. 418-441.

justice and morality as we encounter it in the fifth to the tenth commandments of the decalogue. The alteration of the fifth commandment (namely to honour parents) from a negative to a positive commandment, with its dependence upon forms characteristic of Wisdom literature, carries the process a stage further in the same direction. But in view of the great emphasis which this commandment in particular acquires as a result of being formulated in the affirmative the alteration can perhaps best be understood as the work of a later epoch.

The introduction of the monarchy at first brought with it hardly any basic alterations in the tradition of Israelite justice. As late as the time of Ahab (873-851 BC) the king cannot be permitted to remove a man from his path for no better reason than that he wishes to acquire his vineyard. On the contrary, he has to arrange a sham trial against him with false witnesses for the prosecution. It is only as a result of their evidence that the elders and leading men of the city have Naboth stoned outside it (I Kings 21.1-13). Throughout the entire period of the monarchy justice was the responsibility of the elders of the local communities—at any rate in the cities of the northern kingdom. We may notice that a piece of literary evidence as late, relatively speaking, as Deut. 31.9-13 speaks of an assembly every seven years at the feast of Tabernacles, in which Israel must have the law proclaimed to her. It is perfectly reasonable to regard this as a reflection not only of the conditions prevailing during the period of the judges, but also of those which developed during the period of the monarchy. It is by means of such assemblies that those responsible for administering justice —that is, the elders—gain a deeper knowledge of the actual laws themselves. Moreover these laws are supplemented with fresh material in the course of time. Now there is surely much to be said for the probability that the decalogue may have been coloured at particular points by this sort of living tradition. This is all the more probable in view of the fact that the last five commandments of the decalogue all envisage circumstances which are also covered by the administration of justice at the popular level. The reason given for the third commandment, the prohibition of the misuse of Yahweh's name, might possibly be explained as supporting the theory that the reference is to perjury in the law-court in cases in which a man seeks to defend himself against witnesses for the prosecution.[5]

It may be supposed that the alteration undergone by the prohibition of shedding a neighbour's blood (with the specific purpose of abolishing blood-vengeance) belongs to the end of this period, cf. II Kings 14.5f. Such an attempt to abolish blood-vengeance reflects not only an awareness that times change and milder customs prevail, but also the conviction that the community as a whole cannot endure to suffer loss of strength merely in order to maintain a tradition of the people's distant past. Presumably too the old patriarchal way of life faded away as urban culture developed. Individualism would have come to the fore in the social and economic spheres alike, and a prohibition of stealing a free man from the household of a neighbour would have become more or less irrelevant. In place of this antiquated meaning, therefore, this commandment is taken as the basis for an attempt to condemn first robbery of the poor and plundering by roving bands of brigands, and second the attempts of a new upper class to lay hands upon the possessions of others. The division of the community into proletariat and upper class, especially as this developed in the cities, is the situation presupposed by the existing form of the eighth and tenth commandments. The short formulation of the seventh and eighth commandments may possibly have exercised an influence on the sixth commandment, which could all the more readily be abbreviated in view of the fact that an abbreviation does not necessarily imply an alteration of content. For even in its present shortened formulation the sixth commandment is a prohibition addressed above all to the adult Israelite man with the object of preventing him from intruding upon the marriage of another man.

If the early period of the monarchy was to a certain extent a time of crisis for the customs and usages of ancient Israel, the later period of the monarchy became a time of still greater crisis

[5] Cf. above pp. 100f.

in political, social and religious affairs alike. The reason for this is the expansion of the Assyrian empire towards the West. Israel had already felt some of the effects of this under Omri, Ahab and Jehu, and about the middle of the eighth century BC it became almost catastrophic. For at this time the Assyrians acquired in Tiglath-Pileser III (745-727) a statesman and general of extraordinary power. Within the space of a few years he had crushed the Aramaeans at Damascus, made tributaries of the small states of North Syria and Phoenicia, and subjected the greater part of the kingdom of Northern Israel to Assyrian dominion, dividing it into the three Assyrian provinces of *du'ru*, *makidu* and *gal'azu*, and so incorporating it into his empire. Ten years later Samaria fell after a siege of three years. Ahaz, the king of Judah, came to terms with the Assyrians and by this act the floodgates were opened wide for the Assyrian torrent to pour in over all areas.

Even before the great Assyrian expansion had really commenced Amos, the first of the great prophets, appeared in the northern kingdom; and in the closing years of Israel, when the land was hopelessly torn and divided amid the confusion of power politics, Hosea conducted his mission likewise in the northern kingdom. In the cultural and religious sphere alike these prophets (and this also applies to Isaiah and Micah in the southern kingdom) waged their war on two fronts: against the influence of Assyrian customs and against infiltrations from the side of Canaanite fertility religion. To what extent the prophets may be called pioneers in this struggle is an open question. Earlier investigators were inclined to hold that the emergence of Old Testament ethics and religion was entirely due to the prophets. According to these earlier scholars what the prophets introduced for the first time in Israelite history was 'personal religion'. The research of the last thirty years has caused this theory to be heavily revised. Not least among the factors contributing to this revision are the study of the psalms, the Wisdom literature and the legal material of Israel, as well as that of surrounding cultures. We can now see that the distinctive element in the prophets is not the ethical conception under-

lying their preaching, which finds expression in their de-
nunciations, but the fact that in moments of crisis they stood
forward and, on the basis of that conception of moral principles
which had been handed down to them, pronounced threats of
defeat and destruction precisely at moments when the people
expected to hear promises of victory and good fortune.

Moreover, rightly considered, the prophets did not stand
alone in their struggle against Assyrian influence and against
infiltrations on the part of Canaanite fertility religion. It is precisely to the 'Assyrian period', that is, the period from the
middle of the eighth to the end of the seventh centuries BC, that
most of the laws now available to us in the Holiness Code and
Deuteronomy belong, and what both these collections of laws
have in common is that they are intended, each in its own way,
to shield the true tradition of Israel from foreign influence.
Behind both collections we find circles who live and breathe
in the atmosphere of the old sacral dispensations which have
nothing to do with the state institutions of the period of the
monarchy. In attempting to define these circles more precisely
the Levitical priesthood has been suggested, and we can hardly
arrive at a more satisfactory solution.[6] If our intention was to
attempt to trace the influence of the prophets and Levites in
the history of the decalogue tradition, then we would have to
concentrate our investigation particularly upon the formulation which the first commandment has acquired. It is not only
the phrase *'al pānāy*, 'before my countenance' (which we have
discussed above[7] that makes us say this, but also the expression
'other gods', which is applied to all forms of idolatry, whether
in the form of praying to the national gods of foreign peoples
(one thinks of the history of Solomon, Ahab and Ahaz) or of
the veneration of Canaanite fertility gods, Baal and the 'queen
of heaven'. But the influence of the Levites on the shaping of
the decalogue may possibly have been still greater. We shall

---

[6] On Deuteronomy and the Levites cf. A. Bentzen, *Die josianische Reform und ihre
Voraussetzungen*, 1926, and G. von Rad, *Studies in Deuteronomy*, ET, 1953. On the
Holiness Code' cf. Chr. Feucht, *Untersuchungen zum Heiligkeitsgesetz*, 1962, pp. 179f.
There is a tendency to emphasize the Northern Israelite element in Deuteronomy,
and the Judahite element in the Holiness Code.　　　[7] Cf. pp. 98f. and 121f.

be entering into this question when we define our attitude with regard to the following problems: Is the decalogue an address of Yahweh formulated as a covenant document—for this is certainly more or less how it appears in its final form—or was it from the outset something else, namely a collection of laws which has only acquired the form of a covenant document at a later stage?

6. DIVINE UTTERANCE OR COLLECTION OF LAWS?

The decalogue as known to us in Ex. 20 and Deut. 5 appears as a peculiar mixture of an address by Yahweh and a collection of laws. Even that part of the literary framework which is found in Ex. 20.1, 'And God spoke all these words, saying', serves to emphasize the character of the decalogue as an address of Yahweh. The preliminary presentation of Yahweh in v. 2 has the same effect: 'I am Yahweh your God, who brought you out of the land of Egypt, out of the house of bondage.' As we have seen the first and second commandments are formulated as words spoken by Yahweh. When we come to the third commandment, however, both the commandment itself and the motivating clause that goes with it are, in their present form, a statement of law, and they speak of Yahweh in the third person. Both in the motivating clause and in the rest of the expansions of the sabbath commandment Yahweh is likewise spoken of in the third person. The same applies to the clause in the fifth commandment in which long life is promised to him who honours his parents.

The problem can be stated as follows: as has been shown, a reconstruction of the original form of the decalogue based on form-critical principles opens up two possible ways of understanding the decalogue in terms of literary categories: as direct speech by Yahweh, or as a collection of laws. So far as the original form of the decalogue is concerned it is exclusively the formulation of the third commandment, that concerning the misuse of Yahweh's name, which is the decisive factor in this question. In the secondary additions and modifications we find on the one hand insertions which show that the decalogue was conceived of as an address by Yahweh, on the other insertions which speak of Yahweh in the third person. On the basis of the history of the decalogue tradition as set forth at an earlier stage in our investigation the question might then be raised, 'Which type of additions should be regarded as the earlier?' But there are so many uncertain factors to be allowed for in a judgment based on this sort of comparison that its value is limited. A more fruitful way of putting the question would be 'Could the formulations in the first person represent a modification of supplementary clauses which were originally in the third person?' and conversely, 'Can the formulations in the third person be changed back into a supposedly original formulation in the first?'

To the first of these questions we have already replied in the affirmative.[1] With regard to the second, this too can be answered in the affirmative so far as the third and fifth commandments are concerned. But the fifth commandment does give grounds for reflection, for the reason given, which bears a Deuteronomist stamp, is expressed by a turn of phrase which in Deuteronomy itself is normally formulated in the third person, and is found in the first in only one passage, Deut. 31.20: 'The land which I [Yahweh] swore to give their fathers.' The opposite is true of the additional clauses in the fourth commandment, concerning the sabbath. These are not capable of being turned back into a supposedly original first person form. This is particularly true of the clause giving the reason. If we consider the statement that Yahweh created heaven, earth and sea in six days, rested on the seventh, blessed this day and declared it holy, no one could even dream that this statement could be formulated as an address by Yahweh in the first person. And this serves to indicate that from the outset the decalogue was a collection of laws, and that it was only at a later stage in its tradition that its formulation was changed, so that now it appears as an address by Yahweh—and that only in part.

An argument which points in the same direction can also be

[1] See above, p. 100.

adduced from a comparison between the sabbath commandment as found in the Book of the Covenant, Ex. 23.12, and the
form in which we find it in a quotation from the decalogue in
the Holiness Code, Lev. 19.3. The last-named passage, which
is the later of the two, gives the following version of the sabbath
commandment: 'And you shall keep my sabbaths', whereas in
the Book of the Covenant it runs: 'On the seventh day you shall
observe the sabbath.' Thus the formulation in the first person
appears in the more recent context, while on the other hand the
sabbath commandment in the Book of the Covenant, as with
the rest of the legal statutes contained in the Book of the Covenant, must be understood as the words of the law-giver, that is,
as spoken of Yahweh in the third person.

Now this result has in turn further consequences for our
judgment of the introductory formula, and so also for our ultimate answer to the question of the original setting in life of the
decalogue. Of recent years the Hittite treaty forms have been
adduced again and again[2] as analogies throwing light upon the
introductory formula of the decalogue. For this consists of a
combination of 'preamble' and 'historical prologue', which are
also two integral elements in the Hittite treaty form. In the
preamble the more powerful partner to the pact introduces
himself, and in the historical prologue he rehearses the favours
which he has shown to the one now to become his partner in the
treaty. This is followed by a section setting forth the new conditions of the pact. In the case of the decalogue the self-intro-
duction is represented by the words 'I am Yahweh your God',
and the historical prologue by the words 'who brought you out
of the land of Egypt, out of the house of bondage'. In view of
our foregoing deductions it is immediately evident that no
argument can be drawn from this analogy on which to base a

---

[2] Mendenhall, *Law and Covenant in Israel* . . . 1955. W. Beyerlin, *Origins and
History of the Oldest Sinaitic Traditions*, ET, 1965. K. Baltzer, *Das Bundesformular*,
1960. Most recently A. Kapelrud, 'Some recent points of view on the time and
origin of the Decalogue', *StTh* 18, 1964, pp. 81-90. Walter Zimmerli, the scholar
who has produced the most brilliant analysis of the 'self-presentation' formula and
its advent in Old Testament writing (incidentally the passages are chiefly from the
7th-6th centuries BC!) is far more prudent in drawing historical conclusions. See
especially his essay 'Ich bin Jahve', *Geschichte und Altes Testament*, 1953, pp. 179-209.

definition of the *original* setting in life of the decalogue, still less an argument which justifies the theory of the Mosaic authorship of the decalogue. Let the 'Hittite treaty formula' be as old as it likes. It is only the decalogue in its secondary form, and in its late secondary form at that, which, in respect of this form corresponds to some extent to the pattern of the treaty formula.

As we have seen, the original 'Deuteronomy', which, incidentally, is itself formed as a covenant document, knew nothing of the decalogue. Again the decalogue had originally no place in the ancient traditions of the Sinai covenant as combined with the Book of the Covenant. Finally it must be added that it is precisely the influence of the Deuteronomists which is reflected in the introductory formula, the self-presentation of Yahweh, especially in the description of Egypt as the 'house of bondage'. All things considered we may probably draw the conclusion that Levitical circles such as those known to us from Deuteronomy and the Holiness Code exercised a decisive influence upon the final form of the decalogue. The last stage in the history of the decalogue tradition is the Levitical one. The decalogue finally acquired the status of sacral tradition. But what did it initially emerge as? What circles were responsible for its original composition? If it existed at all in a form resembling, even if only in some degree, the reconstruction which we have attempted to make of it, *when* did it emerge in such a form?

On these questions we shall define our position in the final chapter.

V

THE HISTORICAL PROBLEM
OF THE DECALOGUE

IN the previous chapter we have touched upon the question of *when* the decalogue would probably have been composed, but have not adopted any definite position either on the question of *where* the work of composition might have taken place or as to *what circles* would presumably have been responsible for the composition. These are the three questions which we now propose to treat of in a concluding survey of the whole problem. For this reason we shall once more be discussing the question of what part Moses would have played in the composition of the decalogue. We also propose to raise the further question of what subsequently became of the decalogue, its transformation into a covenant document, and the privileged position which it acquired in the later stages of the Deuteronomist movement. Finally we shall touch very briefly upon the question of the subsequent influence of the decalogue upon Judaism, upon the New Testament and upon the early Church.

I. THE COMPOSITION OF THE DECALOGUE

In the foregoing pages we have rejected the idea that the decalogue would originally have been composed as a covenant document. We have thus placed ourselves in a difficult position in that we have renounced two possibilities which would otherwise have been open to us. First we have renounced the possibility of taking up an otherwise excellent basis for determining more precisely (from a form-critical point of view) the original 'setting in life' of the decalogue. Second we have also foregone the possibility of finding some point of departure for determining the date of the decalogue, i.e. for defining the period of time in which the covenant tradition became a constitutive factor for the Israelite conceptions of religion, community and righteousness as a whole. For instance this might have taken place in the period of Moses or that of the early judges. We have, however, felt convinced of the conclusive validity of that line of thought which tells decisively against the theory that the decalogue would originally have been composed as *sēper habbᵉrīt*, 'a covenant document'. Now therefore, on the basis of the foregoing traditio-historical presentation we must attempt to establish *when* the decalogue was composed, *where* this composition was achieved, and *which circles* may possibly have been responsible for it.

Even in its original form the decalogue betrays a tendency towards synthesis and systematization. We have to thank Albrecht Alt for having demonstrated this by means of a penetrating comparison of the clauses of the decalogue with the various series contained in what he understands to be apodictic law.[1] Regardless of what we may think of Alt's definition of apodictic law, we must nevertheless maintain that a further conclusion to be drawn from such a comparison is that from a form-critical point of view the decalogue cannot be degraded to a mere catechism-like collection of moral precepts. Its affinity to the ancient tradition of justice in Israel is too great for this. In reality what we have in the decalogue is a collection of clauses the binding force of which is more than merely a moral one. In the previous chapter we put forward certain considerations which pointed to the beginning of the period of the monarchy as the probable background for the composition of summary statements of law systematically arranged and aiming at synthesis of the type which we find in the decalogue. The considerations which we then put forward remained at a somewhat general level. Now therefore we shall attempt to give them some substance.

At an earlier stage[2] we pointed out that the introduction

---

[1] Alt, 'Origins . . .', pp. 114-123.   [2] See above, p. 124.

of the monarchy could hardly have meant that the responsibility for law and justice in Israel was taken away from that tribunal which, ever since Israel's settlement on the soil of Canaan, had exercised this responsibility, namely the elders and leading men in the urban communities. Nevertheless another question might be put with regard to the introduction of the monarchy, namely 'How was the monarchy regarded in those circles which were responsible for law and justice in Israel?' We believe that an answer to this question is to be found in two passages in the Old Testament literature, admittedly in a form which bears some mark of the later Deuteronomist movement, whose interest in the monarchy can perhaps best be characterized as 'grown somewhat cooler'. The two passages to which we wish to draw attention are I Sam. 8.10-18 + 10.17-27 and Deut. 17.14-20. It is generally recognized that in their present form these passages represent a vehicle for Deuteronomist ideas, but that the possibility cannot be excluded that the Deuteronomists are here building upon and expanding an ancient tradition.

That the passages in question are indeed relevant to our theme can be seen from the fact that the law of the king in Deut. 17.14-20 is found in the midst of a collection of laws which represents an attempt at a new formulation of the ancient Israelite laws undertaken in the Assyrian period. And the negotiations concerning the introduction of the monarchy which are reflected in the narratives of I Sam. 8 and 10 are carried on between Samuel and 'all the elders of Israel' (8.4) or the representatives of the people who have been summoned to assemble (10.17). Furthermore the passage of I Sam. 10.25 records that in the course of this assembly of the people Samuel declared the *mišpaṭ hammᵉlukā*, 'the law of kingship' to the people and wrote them in a document which was laid up before the countenance of Yahweh, i.e. in a sanctuary. What the aim of this 'law of kingship' was in the existing form of the traditions is revealed with all the clarity that could be desired in I Sam. 8.11ff.: it is a description of the *mišpaṭ hammelek*, 'the right of the king' or better 'the prerogatives of the king.' He can take free Israelites into his service, set up a royal household on a grand scale, exact levies and tithes and in general impose taxes on the property and possessions of the free citizens and upon the fruit of their labours. The connection between these two passages shows that the 'right of kingship' was in reality a kind of 'prophecy' of how the kingship would be degraded once it became fully developed.[3] For when we examine the relevant historical background it becomes apparent that this 'prophecy' is in reality a reflection of Israel's experiences of the monarchy even as early as Solomon's reign. To put it another way: as early as Solomon's reign those who from ancient times had been responsible for law and justice in Israel became aware that the new institution laid claim, in effect, to a large part of that very power which they themselves had been called upon to exercise. That this represents genuine historical memories, and not merely Deuteronomist interpretations, is shown chiefly in the account of the 'local parliament' of Shechem, I Kings 12,[4] in which the resentment of the tribal leaders of Northern Israel at the exaction of forced labour was fanned to a fierce flame. The most striking expression of this resentment was the murder of the task-master Adoniram.

Now let us turn from these passages to the law of the king set forth in Deut. 17.14-20. It is apparent that the ideas expressed here are entirely consonant with the conception of the monarchy in I Sam. 8 and 10. The king, who is to be elected, must be an Israelite. He must not possess many horses, must not send the people back to Egypt, must not take many wives lest he be seduced into apostasy, and he must not amass great wealth of silver and gold. On the positive side he must have a copy of 'this law' made, which he must keep continually beside him, and which he must read assiduously so that he can be

---

[3] It can be established that from the aspect under discussion here this passage has an especially close parallel in the Deuteronomist 'framework' of the Song of Moses in Deut. 32, an element in which, moreover, two originally distinct 'frameworks' have been intermingled, one belonging to the 'prophetic poem' and the other to the law. On this cf. especially Eissfeldt, 'Die Umrahmung des Mose-Liedes Dtn 32.1-43 und des Mose-Gesetzes Dtn 1-30 in Dtn 31.9-32.47', *W.Z. Halle* 4.3, 1955, pp. 411-417.

[4] I have attempted to provide a traditio-historical treatment of this chapter in my work, *Shechem*, 1955, pp. 171-208.

zealous to observe the law, and may increase in fear of the Lord.

As Rabast[5] saw, in the manner in which this law is formulated a certain connection with apodictic law proper is apparent, and this in spite of the use of the third person instead of the second in the prohibitions: *lō' yarbe-lō sūsīm, lō' yarbe-lō nāšīm, lō' yarbe-lō kesep we zāhāb*, 'he must not multiply to himself horses . . . wives . . . silver and gold'. These three clauses, originally so homogeneous in form, together constitute what Rabast calls a 'mirror for the king', and they represent a variant form of the apodictic lists of laws which were compiled and drawn up with some particular area of law or, in this case, with some specific personage in mind. At a later stage Galling subjected this law to a closer analysis,[6] and came to the conclusion that this law of the king is intelligible only in the conditions of the northern kingdom, since only here can there be any question of an elective monarchy. For the Davidic monarchy at Jerusalem was based upon a divine oracle which promised that the House of David would hold dominion in Jerusalem for ever. This 'law of the king', unlike the 'law' in I Sam. 8.11ff., is not a 'prophecy' of how the monarchy will be degraded. Rather it resembles nothing so much as a list of conditions of eligibility composed on the basis of bitter experience under Solomon of what monarchy could mean.

The object of the 'law of the king' was to set firm limits to the development of kingly power, and it is in this very point that it manifests its affinity with the ancient Israelite laws, the original function of which was none other than to provide a sort of 'boundary line'. A law of this sort would have had to be publicly proclaimed as binding at every election of a king, whether the choice fell upon a prince of the royal family or whether another leading Israelite were to be elected with prophetic support.[7]

---

[5] K. Rabast, *Das apodiktische Recht* . . . , 1948, pp. 10f.

[6] K. Galling, 'Das Königsgesetz im Deuteronomium', *TLZ* 76, 1951, cols. 133-138, cf. also Alt, 'Monarchy in the kingdoms of Israel and Judah', ET, *Essays on Old Testament History and Religion*, 1966, pp. 241-59, esp. p. 251.

[7] On the difference in meaning of kingship in Israel from that in Judah cf. Alt's article cited above.

Now we do possess a well authenticated tradition from the earliest period of the monarchy, from the time of David, recording that difficult cases could be brought before the king as to a court of appeal so that the ultimate judgment of a case was left to him (II Sam. 15.1-6). This is the situation which Absalom exploits in order to win over the favour of the Israelite people. The rejection of the Davidic dynasty on the part of the northern kingdom may of course have entailed a change in this connection; attempts may have been made to institute another supreme court of appeal independent of the monarchy.[8] In David's time, however, the power of the supreme court, or the court of appeal, was kept in the hands of the ruler of the united kingdom, and it is most probable that in the subsequent history of the northern kingdom this power was made part of the royal prerogative. This is all the more probable in view of the fact that the traditions of the time of Moses, the memory of which was doubtless most firmly retained and transmitted in northern circles, expressly ascribe this function of supreme judgeship to Moses as leader of the people (Ex. 18.13-27).

It is our thesis, then, that in the northern kingdom not only was this authority regarded as a royal prerogative, but the need was also felt to formulate the fundamental principles on the basis of which judgments were to be arrived at. Hence a 'basic law' was devised as a standard of behaviour for every Israelite, for the Israelite people as a whole, and as a standard for the representative of the Israelite people, its supreme personification, the king. And *this basic law was the decalogue.*

Now while this thesis does provide answers to the question of *when* the decalogue was composed, and also *for what purpose* it was composed, two further questions still remain unanswered, *where* was the compilation of the decalogue undertaken? and by *what circles* was it carried out?

To the first of these two questions we have already replied in a wholly provisional manner by indicating the northern

---

[8] Cf. Noth's theory of an 'office of judge' which would have been in existence throughout the entire history of Israel. Admittedly his point of departure is the book of the Judahite prophet Micah (4.14). Cf. his essay 'Das Amt des Richters', *Festschrift für* A. *Bertholet* 1950, pp. 404ff.

kingdom as the probable place of origin of the decalogue. And in fact the material hardly admits of a more precise answer. We only know that the northern Israelite kingdom in particular was brought into existence by the 'local parliament' which assembled at Shechem after the death of Solomon (I Kings 12). But the Old Testament has nothing which is of relevance to our thesis to tell us about the part subsequently played by this city in the history of the northern kingdom. The most that we can permit ourselves is to draw certain inferences from two passages, namely Deut. 11.29f. and 27.1ff., which offer penetrating insights into the ceremony of sealing the covenant. This is carried out between Mounts Garizim and Ebal, i.e. at ancient Shechem. In the passages concerned the public reading of the law in the presence of all Israel plays an essential part. To suggest, therefore, that Shechem was the place *where* such a basic law would have been composed must remain a hypothesis which in the nature of things can hardly be verified at any time in a wholly definitive manner.

The circles which must presumably have been responsible for the composition of the decalogue can only be such as were in a position, by reason of their most intimate acquaintance with the ancient tradition of law in Israel, to achieve so masterly a summary of it as the decalogue represents. Presumably both the priesthood and the elders would have played a part in this,[9] but in such a manner that in the period during which such a list must have remained in force no opportunity was given for the special interests of the priestly classes to exercise any essential influence upon the subsequent modifications and expansions of the decalogue. Only with the downfall of the monarchy in 722 BC was this opportunity opened up, and, as the foregoing investigations have shown, it was actually taken and used.

[9] The fusion of apodictic and casuistic law in the Book of the Covenant in itself implies that such collaboration between priests and elders must have been practised at a very early date.

2. THE MOSAIC ELEMENT IN THE DECALOGUE

We have dwelt explicitly upon this theme at an earlier stage; here, therefore, we may confine ourselves to a few brief remarks. In our earlier treatment we adopted a decisively hostile position towards the attempts which have been made, both formerly and more recently, to show that the decalogue in some form or another could be—indeed must be—derived from Moses. Our intention was to show that such an assertion implies first that the traditio-historical problems connected with the decalogue have been too lightly passed over, and second that at the historical level it runs counter at certain vital points to the most obvious conclusions, of a kind which follow necessarily from the actual source material of the Old Testament. For all this we have no intention of denying that the genuinely Mosaic tradition really did have an essential contribution to make to the *content* of the decalogue. In this connection we have pointed out that it is the first four commandments, those very ones which, strange to say, have often been adduced as the great obstacle to accepting Mosaic authorship, that are in reality the most easy to understand as embodying the heritage of the wilderness.

This brings us to the consideration of a further aspect. The first four commandments of the decalogue are in reality constitutive for the decalogue as a whole. Now if these first four commandments represent a Mosaic heritage, then again it is only reasonable to seek the origin of the decalogue in a Northern Israelite milieu. For all the traditio-historical factors involved point to the fact that it was in the northern kingdom, the portion of the 'Joseph' tribes, that the Mosaic tradition was most strongly rooted. This must be regarded as a contributing factor lending further support to the theory which we have put forward with particular regard to the decalogue having been composed in the period of the early monarchy in the northern kingdom.

3. THE ADAPTATION OF THE DECALOGUE
AS A COVENANT DOCUMENT

With the downfall of the monarchy and the ruin of the
northern kingdom in 722 BC the decalogue was cut off from its
true background, and this also applies to the 'firm limits' to
kingly power represented by the central nucleus of the Deuteronomist 'law of the king'. We know the process undergone by
the 'firm limits'. They were incorporated in the Deuteronomist
laws, the 'anti-royalist' element in them became intensified
and perhaps at the same time, however paradoxical it may sound,
there was a re-orientation towards the dynastic type of kingship.
For while the concluding clauses of the law of the king (Deut.
17.20) can hardly be understood in any other sense, they become entirely comprehensible precisely in this historical context, that is as expressing the fact that the 'law of the king' has
acquired a fresh application—to the royal house of Judah.

The manner in which the decalogue was introduced into
Deuteronomist circles turns out to be more complex. By reason
of its comprehensive tendency it could not be incorporated in
any one particular section of the Deuteronomist code. We have
put forward the theory that the decalogue owes its origin to the
fact that the king shared in the responsibility of making legal
decisions. Now if this theory is correct then the hesitation with
regard to the decalogue also becomes comprehensible. It is a
reflection of the fact that it was only after the downfall of the
Judahite monarchy that it acquired its definitive position in
the Deuteronomist history writing.

In spite of this, among the Levite circles which stand behind
Deuteronomy the decalogue was taken up and furnished with
the powerful kerygmatic introduction which it now possesses,
and in this way was transformed into a covenant document.
It is not, of course, a literary process that is in question here—
as though there had been a priest acting as writer, re-arranging
the clauses and adding fresh ones. This process is rather one
which was developed in connection with the liturgical activities
of the Levites, their preaching and popular instruction. Such

work as this may well have been carried on at the ancient shrines of the northern kingdom even after Samaria itself had been incorporated as a province in the Assyrian empire. In the Books of Kings we actually find an indication that once the defeated population had been subjected to an initial experience of bloodshed and cruelty, and the numerous mass-deportations had taken place, the Assyrians not merely tolerated the survival of the national religion of Yahweh, but in a sense actually co-operated in its restoration. In the existing text the record of this is to be found in a context which is strongly stamped with the later Deuteronomist attitude of abhorrence towards the cult of the northern kingdom, and with the beginning of the hostility towards the Samaritans. At the same time this context is dominated by the idea that Yahweh can lawfully be worshipped only at a single place, that is, Jerusalem. Within this context the actual passage referred to is the narrative in II Kings 17.24ff., where the legendary story is told of how the population of ancient Samaria were on the point of perishing by reason of the alien forms of cult which they practised. These had been introduced there through the Babylonian and Aramaean elements which had been brought in to settle in the land, and in punishment Yahweh had sent lions among them. Accordingly the people sent a message to the king of Assyria explaining their predicament and bewailing their plight. In reply the king permitted one of the deported Israelite priests to return and establish himself at Bethel in order to instruct the local population there how to worship Yahweh rightly. We believe that an element of historical truth is contained in this legend; in other words, within certain limits the Assyrians allowed and perhaps even encouraged the Israelites who remained behind in the land to practise their religion. For they could be certain that this would not lead to political complications. In Jer. 41.4-10 we possess a unique witness to the fact that genuinely Israelite religious devotion survived in the northern kingdom throughout the period leading to the fall of Jerusalem. In the passage concerned we are told that on the day after the murder of Gedaliah in the year 587 BC eighty pilgrims from Shechem, Samaria and Shiloh passed through Mizpah on their way to Jerusalem. But Ishmael, the murderer of Gedaliah enticed them into the city and then destroyed them. These pilgrims had intended to bring meal offerings and incense to Jerusalem. The fact that Jerusalem was recognized in this way as the religious capital even after its destruction is an eloquent witness of the fact that the law regarding the centralization of the cult, which represents an important stage in the Deuteronomist movement, was by way of finding a response even in the area of what had been the kingdom of Northern Israel.

The development which we have attempted to trace within the area of Northern Israel also exercised an influence upon the kingdom of Judah. This cannot occasion surprise. In the first place, at the time when Samaria fell Judah must have been flooded with refugees from the north who brought with them their own sacral traditions. Second, the political situation in the southern kingdom for the greater part of the seventh century was such that it was easy for the Judahite and Israelite elements in the population to exercise a mutual influence upon each other. The former northern kingdom was divided up into provinces and wholly incorporated in the Assyrian empire. Formally speaking the kingdom of Judah was still independent, but its kings, Manasseh, Amon and Josiah ruled only by favour of the Assyrians, and it was only after the death of Assurbanipal, and the waning of Assyrian power which this implied that the movement for national restoration and independence had any chance at all of free development.

So far as the decalogue is concerned northern influences can be traced in the Holiness Code. A point on which we have touched at an earlier stage is that in the peculiar and somewhat confused collection of apodictic laws contained in Lev. 19[1] we find the decalogue plainly used as a basis for the Levitical

---

[1] In his work, *Das Heiligkeitsgesetz* 1961, pp. 77f. and 162f., Henning Reventlow makes ch. 19 appear to be the central section about which the entire Holiness Code has crystallized. In our lectures at Jerusalem we preferred to regard Lev. 19 as the 'waste paper basket' of apodictic law, although with the proviso that immensely important material can lie concealed in such containers.

preaching which likewise develops wholly within the framework of the old sacral dispensation. It is popular preaching,
priestly 'tora' instruction in the broad sense that we encounter
here[2] with a frequent use of the formula of divine self-presentation: 'I am Yahweh your God.' But this is not used as an introduction, and is not followed, as in the covenant formula, by the
'historical retrospect': '. . . who brought you out of the land of
Egypt.' Instead it is used here to lend further emphasis to the
duty of obeying the law of the jealous God. Here it is the moral
and religious interest that is wholly predominant: the struggle
against pagan customs, the moral concepts derived from ancient
times are here emphasised anew. The juridical affinity which
characterized the decalogue from the outset has here dis-
appeared, a fact which is most clearly illustrated by the
omission of the prohibition of murder and that of adultery.
But here these levitical priests have their own way of conform-
ing themselves to another group of educators within the people
of Judah, namely the sages. At an earlier stage we were concerned with the influence of these sages upon the legal tradition
in the period shortly before the exile.[3] Here we have only one
point to raise. We mentioned that Ps. 19 provides a striking
example of such an influence, and that this influence is revealed
especially in the skill perceptible in this psalm, by which the
full range of all possible variations of expression have been
employed. We find precisely the same trait in the laws of Lev.
19. We are thinking here of the small collection of clauses in
vv. 15-18, culminating in the clause in v. 18b: 'You shall love
your neighbour as yourself.' In these four verses, containing
eleven commandments in all, no less than four, and perhaps
even five different expressions for 'compatriot' have been employed: *'am, re'a, 'aḥ, 'amit* and *ben-'am.* But at this point we
find ourselves straightway in the realm of the subsequent influence of the decalogue.

[2] The use of the second person plural is particularly characteristic of the
priestly 'tora' style.
[3] See above pp. 115ff.

4. THE SUBSEQUENT INFLUENCE OF THE DECALOGUE

The subsequent influence of the decalogue does not derive merely from the privileged position which it acquired in the last decades of the history of the kingdom of Judah. The unique quality inherent in the decalogue itself and in its systematic plan has also been a determining factor, as also has the kerygmatic style which became attached to it in the final phase of its chequered history. In the end it was to acquire a meaning which none of its fathers could have dreamt of. To trace this history in detail would take us too far afield in the realm of Old Testament research. We should have to trace its course through the history of later Judaism to the New Testament, through the early Church and the catechisms of the Middle Ages to the new and ingenious interpretation of the ten commandments in the evangelical spirit put forward by Luther. This work we must leave to others. The area to be covered is wide, and the problems are complicated owing, among other factors, to the many different approaches to the 'problem of law' which we encounter even as early as the New Testament itself. Yet if our presentation of the history of the decalogue in its Old Testament stages can serve to deepen our insight into the problems which are already underwoven with it in the Old Testament, and if such deeper insight can be useful to those who are willing to concern themselves with the further history of the decalogue, then we ourselves will have the satisfaction of knowing that this work can be regarded not merely as a literary or form-critical or traditio-historical investigation, but as a work performed in the service of theology as well.

Abbreviations

ANET	*Ancient Near Eastern Texts Relating to the Old Testament*, ed. J. B. Pritchard, 2nd ed., 1955
ASTI	*Annual of the Swedish Theological Institute*
BA	*The Biblical Archaeologist*
BJRL	*Bulletin of the John Rylands Library*, Manchester
BWANT	Beiträge zur Wissenschaft vom Alten und Neuen Testament
BZ	*Biblische Zeitschrift*
BZAW	Beihefte zur *Zeitschrift für die alttestamentliche Wissenschaft*
cod. A, B, F	codex Alexandrinus, codex Vaticanus, codex Ambrosianus
ET	English translation
FRLANT	Forschungen zur Religion und Literatur des Alten und Neuen Testaments
KHCAT	Kurzer Hand-Commentar zum Alten Testament
Kl. Schr.	Albrecht Alt, *Kleine Schriften zur Geschichte Israels* I-III, 1953-59
LXX	Septuagint
MT	Masoretic Text
NF	Neue Folge
NS	New series
1QS	The Manual of Discipline (from Cave 1 at Qumran)
1QSa	The Rule of the Congregation (from Cave 1 at Qumran)
RB	*Revue Biblique*
SBT	Studies in Biblical Theology
StTh	*Studia Theologica*
TLZ	*Theologische Literaturzeitung*
TR	*Theologische Rundschau*
Tr.	Translator
TZ	*Theologische Zeitschrift*
VT	*Vetus Testamentum*
VTS	*Supplements to Vetus Testamentum*
WMANT	Wissenschaftliche Monographien zum Alten und Neuen Testament
WZHalle	*Wissenschaftliche Zeitschrift der Martin-Luther Universität*, Halle-Wittenberg
ZAW	*Zeitschrift für die alttestamentliche Wissenschaft*

Bibliography

AHARONI, Y., 'Tell Arad'. *RB* 71, 1964, pp. 393-96

ALT, ALBRECHT, 'The Origins of Israelite Law', *Essays on Old Testament History and Religion*, 1966, pp. 79-132
'The Monarchy in Israel and Judah', *ibid.*, pp. 239-59
'Das Verbot des Diebstahls im Dekalog', *Kl. Schr.* I, 1953, pp. 333-40

ANDREW: see STAMM

BAENTSCH, B., *Das Bundesbuch*, 1892

BALTZER, K., *Das Bundesformular* (WMANT 4), 1960

BAUDISSIN, W. W., *Einleitung in die Bücher des Alten Testaments*, 1901

BEER, G., *Steinverehrung bei den Israeliten* (Schriften der Strassburger Wissenschaftlichen Gesellschaft in Heidelberg, NF 4), 1921

BEGRICH, J., 'Die priesterliche Tora', *Werden und Wesen des Alten Testaments* (BZAW 66), 1936, pp. 63-88

BENTZEN, A., *Den israelitiske Sabbats Oprindelse og Historie*, 1923
Die josianische Reform und ihre Voraussetzung, 1926

BENZINGER, I., *Die Bücher der Könige* (KHCAT IX), 1899

BEYERLIN, W., *Origins and History of the Oldest Sinaitic Traditions*, ET, 1965

BOSTRUP, P. O., *Den israelitiske Sabbats Oprindelse og Karakter i foreksilsk Tid*, 1923

BUDDE, K., 'Antwort auf Johannes Meinholds "Zur Sabbathfrage" ', *ZAW* 48, 1930, pp. 138-45

CAZELLES, H., *Études sur le Code de l'Alliance*, 1946

CHARLES, R. H., *The Decalogue*, 1923

CORNILL, C. H., *Einleitung in die kanonischen Bücher des Alten Testaments*, 7th ed., 1913

DIBELIUS, M., *Die Lade Jahves*, (FRLANT 7) 1906

DILLMANN, A., *Die Bücher Exodus und Leviticus*, 2nd ed., 1880

DONNER, H., and RÖLLIG, W., *Kanaanäische und aramäische Inschriften* I-II, 1962-64

DRIVER, S. R., *An Introduction to the Literature of the Old Testament*, 1892

DUHM, B., *Die Psalmen* (KHCAT XIV), 1899

EBERHARTER, A., 'Besitzen wir in Exodus 23 und 34 zwei Rezensionen eines zweiten Dekalogs und in welchem Verhältnis stehen sie zu einander?', *BZ* 20, 1932, pp. 157-62

EERDMANS, B. D., 'Der Sabbath', *Vom Alten Testament: Karl Marti zum 70. Geburtstage gewidmet* (BZAW 41), 1925 pp. 79-83

EISSFELDT, O., 'Die Umrahmung des Mose-Liedes Dtn 32.1-43 und des Mose-Gesetzes Dtn 1-30 in Dtn 31.9-32.47', *WZHalle* 4.3, 1955, pp. 411-17

ELLIGER, K., 'Das Gesetz Leviticus 18' *ZAW* 67, 1955, pp. 1-25

ENGNELL, I., *Gamla Testamentet, En traditionshistorisk Inledning*, 1945
'The Ebed Yahweh Songs and the Suffering Messiah in "Deutero-Isaiah" ', *BJRL* 31, 1948, pp. 54-93
'Herrens Tjänare', *Svenskt Bibliskt Uppslagsverk*, 2nd ed., 1962, pp. 940-43

FEUCHT, C., *Untersuchungen zum Heiligkeitsgesetz* (Theologische Arbeiten 20), 1962

GALLING, K., 'Der Beichtspiegel. Eine gattungsgeschichtliche Studie', *ZAW* 47, 1929, 125-30
'Das Königsgesetz in Deuteronomium', *TLZ* 76, 1951, cols. 133-38

GEHMAN: see MONTGOMERY

GERSTENBERGER, E., *Wesen und Herkunft des sogenannten apodiktischen Rechts im Alten Testament*, 1961

GESE, H., 'Beobachtungen zum Stil alttestamentlicher Rechtsätze', *TLZ* 85, 1960, cols. 147-50

GOETHE, W., *Zwo wichtige, bisher unerörterte biblische Fragen, zum erstenmal gründlich beantwortet. Von einem Landgeistlichen in Schwaben*, 1773 (Goethes Werke. Auswahl in 16 Bänden, Leipzig, Band 7, 1910)

GRESSMANN, H., *Die älteste Geschichtsschreibung und Prophetie Israels* (Die Schriften des Alten Testaments in Auswahl neu übersetzt und für die Gegenwart erklärt), 2nd ed., 1921
Altorientalische Texte zum Alten Testament, 2nd ed., 1926

GRETHER, O., *Name und Wort Gottes im Alten Testament* (BZAW 64), 1934

HAMMERSHAIMB, E., 'On the Ethics of the Old Testament Prophets', *VTS* VII (Congress volume: Oxford 1959), 1960, pp. 75-101

HERRMANN, J., 'Das zehnte Gebot', *Beiträge zur Religionsgeschichte und Archaeologie Palästinas* (Sellin-Festschrift), 1927, pp. 69-82

HOLT, J., *Kilder til Hittiternes Historie*, 1951

HOLZINGER, H., *Exodus* (KHCAT II), 1900

HOSPERS, J. H., *De Numeruswisseling in het Boek Deuteronomium*, 1947

HVIDBERG, F. F., 'Tro og Moral. Den israelitiske Religions Historie', *Haandbog i Kristendomskundskab* II, ed. A. Bentzen, 1943, pp. 204-375

JEPSEN, A., *Untersuchungen zum Bundesbuch* (BWANT Ser. 3, no. 5), 1927

JIRKU, A., *Das weltliche Recht im Alten Testament*, 1927

JOSEPHUS, *Bellum Judaicum* (Loeb Classical Library 203), 1927

KAPELRUD, A. S., 'Some Recent Points of View on the Time and Origin of the Decalogue', *StTh* 18, 1964, pp. 81-90

KLOSTERMANN, A., *Der Pentateuch* I, 1893

KNUDTZON, J. A., *Die El-Amarna Tafeln* (Vorderasiatische Bibliothek II.1), 1915

KOCH, K., 'Tempeleinlassliturgien und Dekaloge', *Studien zur Theologie der alttestamentlichen Überlieferungen* (G. von Rad zum 60. Geburtstag), 1961, pp. 45-60

KOEHLER, L., 'Der Dekalog', *TR*, NF 1, 1929, pp. 161-84

KOHLER, J., and PEISER, F. E., *Hammurabi's Gesetz* I, 1904

KOSMALA, H., 'The so-called Ritual Decalogue', *ASTI* 1, 1962, pp. 31-61

LIE, A. G., *Gamle assyriske Love*, 1924

LODS, A., *Histoire de la littérature hébraïque et juive*, 1950

MEIER, E., *Die ursprüngliche Form des Dekalogs*, 1846

MEINHOLD, J., 'Die Entstehung des Sabbats', *ZAW* 29, 1909, pp. 81-112 *Der Dekalog*, 1927
    'Zur Sabbathfrage', *ZAW* 48, 1930, pp. 121-38

MENDENHALL, G. E., *Law and Covenant in Israel and the Ancient Near East*, 1955

MINETTE DE TILESSE, G., 'Sections "tu" et sections "vous" dans le Deuteronome', *VT* 12, 1962, pp. 29-88

MONTGOMERY, J. A., and GEHMAN, H. S., *The Books of Kings* (International Critical Commentary), 1951

MOWINCKEL, S., *Psalmenstudien V, Segen und Fluch in Israels Kult und Psalmdichtung*, 1924
    De tidligere Profeter (Det gamle Testamente, oversatt af Michelet, Mowinckel og Messel, II), 1935
    Le Décalogue, 1927
    'Zur Geschichte der Dekaloge', *ZAW* 55, 1937, pp. 218-35
    Offersang og Sangoffer, 1951; ET, *The Psalms in Israel's Worship*, 1962

NICOLSKY, N. M., 'Das Asylrecht in Israel', *ZAW* 48, 1930, pp. 146-75

NIELSEN, E., *Shechem. A Traditio-historical Investigation*, 1955
    'The Burial of the Foreign Gods', *StTh* 8, 1954, pp. 103-22
    'Some Reflections on the History of the Ark', *VTS* VII (Congress volume: Oxford 1959), 1960, pp. 61-74
    'La Guerre considerée comme une religion et la Religion comme une guerre', *StTh* 15, 1961, pp. 93-112

NOTH, M., *Das System der zwölf Stämme Israels* (BWANT, Ser. 4, no. 1), 1930
    ' "For All who Rely on Works of the Law are under a Curse" ', *The Laws in the Pentateuch and Other Essays*, ET, 1966, pp. 118-31
    'The Laws in the Pentateuch', *op. cit.*, pp. 1-107

Überlieferungsgeschichtliche Studien I (Schriften des Königsberger Gelehrten Gesellschaft, geist. wiss. Klasse 18), 1943
Überlieferungsgeschichte des Pentateuchs, 1948
'Das Amt des Richters Israels', *Festschrift für A. Bertholet*, 1950, pp. 404ff.

PEDERSEN, J., *Israel: its Life and Culture*, III-IV, ET, 1940

PEISER: see KOHLER

PFEIFFER, R. H., *Introduction to the Old Testament*, 1941

PHILO, *De Decalogo* (Loeb Classical Library 320), 1937

RABAST, K., *Das apodiktische Recht im Deuteronomium und im Heiligkeitsgesetz*, 1948

RAD, G. VON, *The Problem of the Hexateuch and Other Essays*, ET, 1966
Studies in Deuteronomy, ET (SBT 9), 1953
Genesis, ET (Old Testament Library), 1961
' "Gerechtigkeit" und "Leben" in der Kultsprache der Psalmen', *Festschrift für A. Bertholet*, 1950, pp. 418-37
'Die Anrechnung des Glaubens zur Gerechtigkeit', *TLZ* 76, 1951, cols 129-32
Old Testament Theology I, ET, 1962

REVENTLOW, H., *Das Heiligkeitsgesetz* (WMANT 6), 1961
Gebot und Predigt im Dekalog, 1962

ROWLEY, H. H., 'Moses and the Decalogue', *BJRL* 34, 1951, pp. 81-118

RÖLLIG: see DONNER

RUDOLPH, W., *Der 'Elohist' von Exodus bis Josua* (BZAW 68), 1938

SCHMIDT, H., 'Mose und der Dekalog', *Eucharisterion* (Gunkel-Festschrift; FRLANT 36) I, 1923, pp. 78-119

SCHWALLY, F., *Der heilige Krieg im alten Israel*, 1901

STAMM, J. J., 'Sprachliche Erwägungen zum Gebot "Du sollst nicht töten" ', *TZ* 1, 1945, pp. 81-90
'Dreissig Jahre Dekalogforschung', *TR*, NF 27, 1961, pp. 189-239 and 280-305

STAMM, J. J., and ANDREW, M. E., *The Ten Commandments in Recent Research*, ET (SBT NS 2), 1967

STAERK, W., *Das Deuteronomium, sein Inhalt und seine literarische Form*, 1894

STEUERNAGEL, C., *Die Rahmen des Deuteronomiums*, 1894
Lehrbuch der Einleitung in Das Alte Testament, 1912

SZLECHTER, E., 'Le code d'Ur-nammu', *Revue d'Assyriologie* 49, 1955, pp. 169-77

VAUX, R. DE, *Ancient Israel: its Life and Institutions*, ET, 1961

WELLHAUSEN, J., *Prolegomena to the History of Israel*, ET, 1885, reprinted 1962

Die Composition des Hexateuchs und der historischen Bücher des alten Testaments, 2nd impression, 1889

WRIGHT, G. E., 'Solomon's Temple at Jerusalem', *BA* 4, 1941, pp. 17-31

ZIMMERLI, W., 'Ich bin Jahve', *Geschichte und Altes Testament* (Festschrift für A. Alt. Beiträge zur historische Theologie 16), 1953, pp. 179-209

Ezechiel (Biblische Kommentar, Altes Testament 13), 1958ff.

The Law and the Prophets, ET, Oxford, 1965, New York, 1967

Indexes

Index of Subjects

Index of Authors

Index of Biblical References